CHANGE IN THE CHILEAN COUNTRYSIDE

Also by David E. Hojman

CHILE: The Political Economy of Development and Democracy in the 1990s
CHILE AFTER 1973: Elements for the Analysis of Military Rule (*editor*)
DESARROLLO REGIONAL Y PLANIFICACION REGIONAL
ECONOMIC MODELS OF LATIN AMERICA (*editor with A. Cordery*)
NEO-LIBERAL AGRICULTURE IN RURAL CHILE (*editor*)

Change in the Chilean Countryside

From Pinochet to Aylwin and Beyond

The Proceedings of the 46th International Congress of Americanists, Amsterdam, Holland

Edited by

David E. Hojman

Senior Lecturer in Economics and Latin American Studies
Institute of Latin American Studies
University of Liverpool

M

First published 1993 by
THE MACMILLAN PRESS LTD
Houndmills, Basingstoke, Hampshire RG21 2XS
and London
Companies and representatives
throughout the world

ISBN 0–333–55050–1

A catalogue record for this book is available
from the British Library.

Printed in Great Britain by
Antony Rowe Ltd
Chippenham, Wiltshire

Contents

List of Tables and Figures

Tables

Figures

Preface

In the Summer of 1988, María Elena Cruz and Rigoberto Rivera, from the Grupo de Investigaciones Agrarias (GIA), Universidad Academia de Humanismo Cristiano, Santiago, and David E. Hojman, from the Department of Economics and Institute of Latin American Studies (ILAS), University of Liverpool, jointly organised a workshop on 'Neo-liberal Policies, Agriculture and Social Change in Chile', in the context of the 46th International Congress of Americanists (ICA) in Amsterdam.

The present book is the second volume of a set of two, both based on extensively revised, extended and actualised versions of the papers originally presented to the above workshop. The first volume (*Neo-liberal Agriculture in Rural Chile*, edited by David E. Hojman, London: Macmillan, 1990) was fundamentally concerned with the changes in Chilean agriculture and rural society resulting from the neo-liberal policies implemented by the military regime of General Augusto Pinochet between 1973 and 1990. The present volume takes as its starting point the material presented in the first volume, but its main concern is a rather different one. Its subject is, first, the period of political transition between the authoritarian Pinochet regime and the first democratic administration inaugurated in 1990, headed by the Christian Democrat Patricio Aylwin; and, secondly, the prospects for the later 1990s. In the present book we deal with the prospects for democratic agricultural development in the 1990s. We intend to look at how the inheritance of the policies from the 1970s and 1980s will determine the options available to policymakers in the new democratic era, but we also go far beyond that. As a result of the Pinochet regime, Chile has changed beyond recognition. In this volume we look at the promises and threats behind this new face of the country, and at the parallel needs for continuity and for change which will inevitably mark agricultural development in the future.

The Chilean attempts at transforming agriculture and the economy along neo-liberal lines in the 1970s and 1980s were unprecedented in their energy and, together with the 1990s' efforts at generating a just and economically dynamic society under conditions of political democracy by using market mechanisms inherited from the previous regime, are possibly unique in the developing world. In this sense other Latin American countries and Third World nations possibly have much to learn from both the successes and the failures of the Chilean experience.

Several of the chapters published in the present book were improved by the discussion of preliminary versions in a number of scholarly meetings. The authors wish to record their gratitude towards the participants in the following venues: the Chile Workshop in the 1988 Amsterdam Congress, the GIA–CLACSO International Conference on Latin American Agriculture, Punta de Tralca, Chile, 1988; the annual Conference of the British Society for Latin American Studies, Jesus College, Oxford, 1990; the CERC–ILAS–St Antony's College Conference on the Transition to Democracy in Chile, University of Liverpool, 1990; the International Conference on Agricultures and Peasantries in Latin America: Mutations and Recompositions, University of Toulouse-le-Mirail, Toulouse, 1990; and the Workshop on 'Economy and Society in Chile after Neo-liberalism', at the 47th International Congress of Americanists (ICA), New Orleans, 1991.

The editor wishes to thank his co-organisers in Amsterdam, María Elena Cruz and Rigoberto Rivera, and the heads of the respective institutions, GIA and ILAS Liverpool, Cecilia Leiva and John Fisher. He is also grateful to the other authors in both volumes, and to Jorge Hojman, Luis Kaffman, Patrick Minford, Richard Morris, Peter Vandome and Bob Wynn, for their ideas, advice, encouragement and patience. Last but not least, very special thanks are due to the Committee of the 46th International Congress of Americanists in Amsterdam, who provided a generous grant to help with the costs of publication of this book. Without their splendid support this volume would have not been possible.

Institute of Latin American Studies
University of Liverpool   DAVID E. HOJMAN

Notes on the Contributors

Anna Bee is a PhD candidate in the Department of Geography, University of Birmingham.

Julio A. Berdegué is an agronomist and a former senior researcher in the Grupo de Investigaciones Agrarias (GIA), Santiago. He now works at the Chilean office of the Interamerican Institute for Cooperation on Agriculture (IICA).

Shanti P. Chakravarty is Senior Lecturer in Economics, Department of Economics, University College of North Wales, Bangor, Gwynedd.

María Elena Cruz is an agrarian economist. She is now a senior researcher and Deputy Director of the Grupo de Investigaciones Agrarias (GIA), Santiago.

Guy Durand is Lecturer in Agricultural Economies, Department of Economic and Social Sciences, Ecole National Supérieure Agronomique, Rennes.

Robert N. Gwynne is Lecturer in Latin American Development, Department of Geography, University of Birmingham.

David E. Hojman is Senior Lecturer in Economics, Department of Economics and Institute of Latin American Studies, University of Liverpool.

Cristóbal Kay is Senior Lecturer in Rural Development Studies, Institute of Social Studies (ISS), The Hague.

Carlo Pietrobelli is a PhD candidate in Oxford University, and a Lecturer at the Department of Economics and Institutions, University of Rome, 'Tor Vergata'.

Rigoberto Rivera is a former senior researcher in the Grupo de Investigaciones Agrarias (GIA), Santiago. He is now at the Latin American Faculty of Social Sciences (FLASCO), Brasilia.

Christopher D. Scott is Lecturer in Economics, Department of Economics, London School of Economics and Political Science (LSE).

Patricio Silva is Lecturer in the Political Sociology of Latin America, Institute of Cultural and Social Studies, Leiden University.

Acknowledgements

The editor and publishers wish to thank the following for permission to reproduce copyright material:

Unwin Hyman, for Table 2.1, from L.S. Jarvis, 'The unraveling of Chile's agrarian reform, 1973–1986', in W.C. Thiesenhusen (ed.), *Searching for Agrarian Reform in Latin America* (1989).

Croom Helm, for Table 3.8, from W.C. Labys and P.K. Pollak, *Commodity Models for Forecasting and Policy Analysis* (1984).

Introduction
David E. Hojman

The present volume is devoted to analysing the ways in which economic and social changes in the Chilean countryside in recent decades – and in particular during the 1970s and 1980s, under the authoritarian rule of General Augusto Pinochet – are likely to affect the future course and nature of agricultural development, economic growth, and the political transition to democratic rule in the 1990s. We are also interested in the ways in which agrarian policies in the 1990s are likely to reflect previous developments, and to differ from the policies of previous decades, and on how this will affect present and future patterns of agricultural development. This volume does not, as its central concern, look at the Pinochet neo-liberal policies in the countryside, and their results, because this has already been attempted elsewhere (Hojman, 1990). What we intend to examine here are rather the promises and dangers of democratic agricultural development in the 1990s. This obviously requires that attention should be paid to the inheritance from the authoritarian period, but it also implies going far beyond it. The Introduction presents the principal arguments and conclusions of individual chapters, and aims to suggest some links between these chapters. But both the general conclusions and further examination of some recurrent themes and questions are left for Chapter 11 of this book.

The principal successes and failures of the neo-liberal experiment in agriculture are concisely but systematically presented by María Elena Cruz in Chapter 1, 'Neo-liberal Agriculture and Democratisation'. The successes refer basically to economic performance; the failures, to its social and political costs. During the 1970s and 1980s, there were also a number of complex global changes: in the economic, geographical, social, political, and demographic spheres. It would be difficult to catalogue these changes as 'good' or 'bad', but they are clearly permanent, or 'structural'. They resulted from the Pinochet policies, but no amount of policy reversals, even if attempted (which may not be among the aims of the Aylwin or future administrations), could manage to reverse these effects. With regard to democratisation, Cruz is not optimistic. She sees the prospects for the new

1

democratic governments in the 1990s as difficult. According to her, the main victims of the 1980s' model were the landless wage labourers. Top priority should be granted to the restoration and preservation of democracy, which will inevitably require some significant redistribution of wealth and income, even if this may entail some cost in terms of production targets. Making growth and equity compatible, in a democratic context in which the victims of the neo-liberal model are allowed freely to express their demands, will not be easy. Instability in international markets, the limitations to the possibilities for expanding domestic demand, the marginalisation of peasants, the danger of potential riots, land invasions and other forms of social explosion, and the insensitivity of rural employers to their workers' plight, are unlikely to help. This chapter ends with an invitation to design and implement policies according to the needs and creativity of the people, rather than by following ideologies and textbook paradigms.

In reply to the central question posed by Chapter 2, 'The Agrarian Policy of the Aylwin Government: Continuity or Change?', Cristóbal Kay argues that there is continuity in economic policy, but change in terms of the social emphasis. Aylwin's attempts at moving towards a 'neo-liberal model with a human face' would represent the definitive consolidation of the late 1960s' right-wing Christian Democrat model of President Eduardo Frei for capitalist development in the countryside. Kay highlights the relative stabilisation of the structure of land tenure after the land reform and counter-reform upheavals, the final and complete separation of the traditional peasant family from their land, and the export boom, as the three principal aspects of the modernisation of agriculture under Pinochet. The creation of rural land and labour markets, for all its costs in human terms, is a manifestation of progress, of the fact that return to the traditional *hacienda* system is now impossible. But the credit for starting this process of modernisation belongs to Frei. Aylwin's objective, in the midst of a rural environment of 'modernising fever', would be not to eliminate Pinochet's 'savage capitalism', but to tame it by introducing a 'peasantist bias' into it. The principal characteristics of the Aylwin agrarian policies would be a commitment to the market economy and to exports, technological support with emphasis on peasant farmers, expenditure in social services against poverty, price support to crops for the domestic market, reforms to the labour and local government laws, strengthening the state apparatus, and reduction of the farmers' debt. The most difficult task may well prove to be improving the lot of poor peasants.

Given the almost undiluted commitment to markets in the agricultural policies of both the Pinochet and Aylwin administrations, against all the recommendations of the export pessimism school, it may be advisable to examine some of the implicit and explicit assumptions behind typical arguments for and against reliance on the operation of markets. Shanti P. Chakravarty in Chapter 3, 'Agriculture and Forestry: Reflections on Liberal Policies', looks at issues concerning world price instability in agricultural commodity trade, and at questions dealing with the environment, cost–benefit decisions and inter-generational equity in the case of forestry. Opting for a strategy with a low expected return and a low variance in this expected return – and therefore a low risk (such as food production for self-consumption, or import-substituting industrialisation) – makes economic sense compared with alternatives yielding higher expected returns with high return variances (such as export specialisation according to comparative advantage), only if the capital or insurance markets are imperfect. Supporters of food self-sufficiency also use the national security argument (examples of this are provided in Silva's Chapter 4). But Chakravarty maintains that the Chilean strategy of emphasis on agricultural exports made sense, even during the credit-starved 1980s, not only because international agricultural prices are no more volatile than the prices of metals and minerals, but also because the particular Chilean combination of traditional mineral and non-traditional agricultural exports of the late 1980s and early 1990s represented a composite export price which was more stable than either of the other price series. The picture presented by forestry is less favourable. And this is not a question of degree, the difference being qualitative rather than quantitative. So far no effort has been made to deal with forestry's negative externalities, inflicted upon either current or future generations. The latter in particular involve questions, some of them related to distributive justice, which have not yet even been asked, let alone answered in any depth.

Patricio Silva in Chapter 4, 'Landowners and the State: Beyond Agrarian Reform and Counter-reform', explores some historical aspects of the development of the principal associations of agrarian entrepreneurs, from the early 1960s, when land reform started, to the present. It emerges that the attitudes of rural landowners towards the military regime were a mixture of gratitude and conflict, the latter deriving from the landowners' pressures to secure some protectionist measures in their favour (the cases of wheat and milk are representative). Academics' and social scientists' perceptions of who the agrarian entrepreneurs are, or were, have changed substantially. During the 1960s, large landowners were seen as backward, traditional, even 'pre-capitalist'. They were presented as a barrier to output expansion and social justice in the countryside and in society as a whole – this despite the fact that, as acknowledged by Silva, a large share of rural landowners were even then modern, dynamic entrepreneurs. By contrast, 20, 25 or 30 years later, agricultural employers are considered to be among the most dynamic forces in society (this point is also made by Cristóbal Kay in Chapter 2). But this change in perceptions may be explained in several alternative ways. Either landowners have changed, or social scientists have, or the fabric of society has been altered, or any combination of these possibilities has occurred. Possibly all of the above have indeed happened, at the same time, as all the old actors have been replaced by a new generation.

Chapter 5, 'The Sugar Beet Industry: A Model for Agricultural Self-sufficiency in a Developing Country?', by Robert N. Gwynne and Anna Bee, examines the IANSA (*'Industria Azucarera Nacional'*) programme for domestic sugar production using domestically produced sugar beet. According to certain criteria, the programme is a success. The country is now self-sufficient in sugar. Sugar beet grows well in many Chilean regions, including dry, non-irrigated coastal areas, and the opportunity cost of using this land is quite small. Beet yields in the late 1980s were among the highest in the world, and unit costs of beet sugar production in IANSA factories were among the lowest. However, despite all this, sugar produced from Chilean beet is still more expensive than that produced from, for example, Argentine sugar cane. The IANSA programme can survive only if protected by high tariff barriers against imports. The programme is an import substitution one, and as such it possibly would not have been designed and implemented if the 1982–3 crisis had never happened, or if the spectacular collapse of CRAV (the

'*Compañía Refinadora de Azúcar de Viña del Mar*') had not played such a notorious role in the preliminary stages of development of the crisis. For all practical purposes beet farmers act almost exactly as profit-sharing IANSA employees. Both a monopolist and a monopsonist, IANSA provides seed, fertiliser, pesticide, equipment, credit and technical advice, and it guarantees a market for the product. Among other things, the IANSA beet programme shows that given the proper conditions, even the poorest farmer with the worst land can behave successfully as a profit-maximising agent. How much has society to pay for this triumph is another matter.

High levels of efficiency in production, even up to the point of reaching international standards of competitiveness in non-traditional exports, did not require tariffs or other conventional forms of government protection. This is one of the messages of Chapter 6, by Carlo Pietrobelli, on 'Non-traditional Agricultural and Agro-industrial Exports and Technological Change: A Micro-economic Approach'. On the other hand, this does not mean that all forms of government intervention are negative or useless. On the contrary, an active role for government may be essential in dealing with frequent instances of market failure in the technology markets, and in contributing to the formation of skilled personnel by investing in human capital. Pietrobelli shows that the neoclassical approach offers little help in understanding the generation of dynamic comparative advantages, and consequently adopts an eclectic theoretical framework, which is then tested by applying it to a small sample of successful non-traditional exporters. Evidence is presented that the firm is the relevant unit of development of dynamic comparative advantage; that, in addition to a sympathetic and stable macroeconomic environment, large natural resources and a cheap and effective labour force, technological capabilities are required; that the latter often consist of the capacity to identify the need for, and then design and carry out, small changes or even apparently insignificant modifications in equipment, processes, the product, or even packing, marketing and certification techniques, most of which are typically ignored by the traditional theory; and that technological capabilities are frequently developed or improved with support from government or semi-official agencies, foreign trade intermediaries or final consumers abroad.

Chapters 7–10 are devoted to analysing different aspects of the situation of the peasantry, and examining several efforts to improve their lot. Christopher D. Scott in Chapter 7, 'Rural Credit, Agricultural Extension and Poverty Alleviation: Past Experience and Future Prospects', starts by examining the evolution of the extent of poverty in rural areas between the second half of the 1960s and the second half of the 1980s, and the contribution being made to its alleviation by the credit and technical support policies of the Institute of Agricultural Development, INDAP (*Instituto de Desarrollo Agropecuario*). Scott is in the highly favourable position (possibly unique by developing country standards) of being able to compare results from surveys carried out with a 20-year interval, upon the same peasant population sample. Despite the very significant differences in the overall circumstances surrounding these two periods, he observes the presence of fundamental continuities in terms of a statistically significant, positive association between access to formal credit (which was both subsidised and rationed) and the use of inputs such as chemical fertiliser and improved seeds. The respective associations of credit access with the use of insecticide, herbicide and fungicide are less strong. In the first period there was also a strong positive association between exposure to INDAP extension activities and the use of INDAP as a source of problem solving. These statistical results are discussed in the context of several important hypotheses. This chapter concludes with a proposition for the creation of local Rural Development Committees, which should play an essential role in generating and encouraging grassroots participation, something so far beyond the possibilities of central government agencies, local government, or non-governmental organisations (NGOs) in rural areas.

Despite the fact that peasant farming experienced some yield increases in the 1970s and 1980s, the technological gap between medium-sized and large scale commercial farming on the one hand, and peasant farming on the other, was by the beginning of the 1990s worse than ever before. The widest yield gaps appear precisely in the productions of crops which have recently seen substantial technical progress. Gaps in yields, especially in some regions, are so large that the most accurate description of peasant activity there is possibly 'marginalisation'. Guy Durand in Chapter 8, 'Agricultural Policies, Technological Gap, and

Peasant Farming: From Pinochet to Aylwin', reviews the Pinochet regime programmes of technological support for farmers. He concludes that the specific characteristics of these programmes contributed significantly to worsening the technological gap. Each programme was clearly addressed to a different stratum of the rural population, but all of them failed to reach more than a small fraction of their intended targets. The Aylwin government aimed at devoting most resources in the agricultural budget to the support of peasants and poor farmers through INDAP, but budget constraints meant that it would have to rely on subcontracting work from private sector extension firms, and on NGOs. Problems of methodology, training of rural development officials, and participation by the beneficiaries themselves, remain unresolved. According to Durand, a key role for the price system should be maintained, but this role should also be limited by structural boundaries and definitions. Peasant development should be pursued not only or mainly because there is a 'social debt' owed to peasants, but essentially because the greatest potential for productive expansion lies with them.

A combination of the policies of the Pinochet regime, a massive supply of unemployed skilled personnel and returning exiles from abroad with experience in government agricultural organisations before 1973, substantial financial support from international agencies, and widespread poverty in rural areas, all came together to stimulate the development of a large and heterogeneous collection of non-governmental organisations (NGOs, or ONGs, *organizaciones no gobernamentales*). Julio A. Berdegué in Chapter 9, 'Non-governmental Development Programmes for the Peasant Sector: A Critical Review' admits that these entities failed in several respects, when their performance is assessed using their own exacting standards. Their heterogeneity makes it difficult to generalise, and the harshest criticism may not apply to all NGOs, but still some conclusions are possible. First, they failed in their aim of offering a model of agricultural development 'alternative' to the one presented by the military regime. Ideally this alternative model should have been cooperative, or somehow 'not capitalist', and should have promoted values such as peasant dignity and solidarity. NGOs also failed in terms of offering new, different technological options, be they 'intermediate', 'appropriate', or 'organic'. And even their attempts at improving the material living and production conditions of those participating in their programmes were not successful. NGOs were unable to organise and coordinate between themselves when several of them were operating in the same geographical region, were unable to resist the temptation of following irrelevant 'fashions', and were unable to understand or interpret the actual needs and aspirations of peasants, and the trends in domestic and international agriculture. However, despite this sorry picture, they trained staff, kept hopes alive, and allowed pockets of grassroots participation and democratic decision-making.

The victims of the neo-liberal model in rural areas, poor peasants and landless rural labourers, have developed a multiplicity of forms of organisation in order to survive. This is the subject of Chapter 10, by Rigoberto Rivera, 'Self-help Organisations and Non-governmental Programmes of Rural Development'. Among these self-help units we find soup kitchens, first aid chests, community health groups, peasant committees, craft production workshops, workshops for mending second-hand clothes, informal credit unions, housing agencies, vegetable garden committees, basic training schemes, and so on. Some of these self-help units derive from peasant unions or other organisations from the land reform period and may still be connected to them. Most self-help units cannot survive without permanent support from a NGO or from the Church. Self-help organisations lack their own growth dynamics and they do not generate enough income to become substitutes for capitalist agriculture or to prevent migration. Men decline to participate in these entities and they are not keen to see women participating. Since NGOs have been unable to make self-help units independent from NGO support, this is in fact another example of the rural NGOs' failure to generate a pattern of 'alternative' or autonomous development. Rivera believes that NGOs have coherent theories, but find it difficult to relate these theories to their actual practice of rural development. He suggests that NGOs' romantic notions of peasant solidarity and cooperation should be abandoned.

Chapter 11, 'Continuity, Legitimacy, and Agricultural Development: Conclusions', by the editor, reviews the general conclusions of the volume, paying particular attention to macroeconomic balance and the importance of policy; the international economy and relations with the largest importer, the

United States; quality control; exports of fruit, forestry, wine, and other non-traditional exports; protection granted to domestic agriculture and agro-industry; the question of equity in government expenditure; the labour market; and the issue of poverty.

Reference

Hojman, D. E. (ed.)(1990) *Neo-liberal Agriculture in Rural Chile* (London: Macmillan).

1 Neo-liberal Agriculture and Democratisation
María Elena Cruz

1.1 SUCCESSES OF THE NEO-LIBERAL MODEL

The neo-liberal model's successes in rural areas are basically related to export growth, modernisation in the cultivation of basic foodstuffs by commercial producers, investment in plantations and agro-industry, and the inflows of foreign capital addressed in particular to the forestry and fruit sectors.

The area planted with forestry and fruits has expanded considerably. Between 1973 and 1986 the area planted with fruit trees doubled, to reach 130 000 hectares. The Central Valley (Aconcagua to Curicó) share of this total was 84 per cent. Plantations of radiata pine, which are both highly subsidised and the principal source of forestry exports, are about 1 million hectares, compared with about 200 000 in 1965–73.

This increase in planting has not been matched by that in the so-called 14 basic foodstuffs, which have experienced large fluctuations. In the period 1965–75 they represented about 1 200 000 hectares, which fell to 870 000 hectares in 1982–3, to recover to historical levels by the late 1980s.

However, average yields in basic foodstuffs increased substantially after 1984, as a result of corrective measures adopted after the crisis. In eight out of 14 foodstuffs, yields increased between 50 and 70 per cent from 1979–80 to 1985–6. This increase was basically experienced by commercial producers, since peasants were much more slow at catching up with new technological advances.

The use of inputs has increased. This is reflected in sales of fertilisers and imports of pesticides. Sales of nitrate, the most frequently used nitrogen fertiliser, trebled between 1980 and 1985, and those of phosphate rose by 40 per cent. Imports of pesticides, which to a large extent go to fruit produced for export markets, increased from 6 million dollars in 1977 to 25 million in 1983 and 50 million in 1987.

The dramatic increase in exports in just a matter of a few years is another achievement. The total formed by agriculture and forestry exports rose from 250 million dollars in 1974 to over 1300 million in 1987. In 1980 these exports were the equivalent of only about one-quarter of the value of copper exports, against 65 per cent in 1987 (when the copper price was particularly high). As a share of total exports, agriculture and forestry represented 27 per cent in 1987.

There are no figures for total or agro-industrial investment, but the high rates of return in the sector have generated more planting, investment in new technologies and varieties, purchase of equipment, and new building. These investments are apparent and for years their dynamism contrasted with the relative stagnation of investment in urban industry.

The impact of individual factors in this agricultural revival is difficult to determine, but possibly they can be divided into three groups: financial, higher profitability, and diffusion of technological progress.

When the Pinochet regime noted that export revenues were being addressed overwhelmingly towards food imports, a decision to diversify the sources of foreign exchange generation and savings was taken. Price stability and profitability were guaranteed to producers of some basic foodstuffs by establishing price bands. Tariffs were selectively raised from a uniform 11 per cent to 20 and then 35 per cent, and finally settled at 30 per cent. Renegotiation of the large domestic debt of agricultural producers, estimated at 1500 million dollars in 1984, led to more generous terms. A programme of agricultural extension addressed to large producers was successful: those favoured expanded from 13 groups with 233 farmers in 1982 to 120 groups with 1855 farmers in 1985. This represented about 750 000 hectares.

Since 1985, gross domestic product in agriculture has been growing consistently at a faster rate than global GDP.

1.2   EFFECTS IN RELATION TO POVERTY

According to some estimates, 3.6 million people, one-third of the population, were destitute (or indigent, or in extreme poverty) in 1983. This means that they could not afford a basic food basket (the respective figure for 1970 was 6 per cent). In rural areas

destitution may have affected as many as 50 per cent of the
population, although analysts admit that this calculation does
not take production for self-consumption into account. Of
course, there were many who could afford the basic food basket,
but little else.

Several reasons help to explain why the rural poor suffered
from the application of the neo-liberal model. The first is the
state's withdrawal from its traditional roles in productive support, cheap loans, free technical assistance, training, and support
to investment in and outside peasant plots. Massive support
programmes have been replaced by partial and selective ones.
This is reflected in the elimination of the state machinery in
agriculture, which amounted to 23 000 jobs in December 1973.
INDAP, the Institute of Agricultural Development, oriented
towards the peasant sector, employed almost 4000 people. By
1979 the state agricultural payroll had fallen to 7000, and that of
INDAP to slightly over 1000. There is no direct correlation
between the number of officials and state efficiency, but at least
the numbers give us some idea about the government's intentions towards the peasant sector.

Other indicators are provided by land ownership, peasant
organisations, living conditions, minimum wages, social security, and access to housing. More than half of those peasants or
labourers who received land from expropriated farms after the
land reform and counter-reform experiences (the *parceleros*) have
had to sell their plots under unfavourable terms. In 1973 there
were 300 peasant cooperatives, but by 1982 only about 70 of
them survived. In particular after 1987, the Pinochet government engaged in a 'National Plan of Rural Development', which
aimed at improving living conditions in rural areas, but this
initiative, despite some successes, was interpreted by those in
charge of applying it as being incompatible with the organisation
of, and participation by, beneficiaries.

Those most negatively affected by the neo-liberal model in the
countryside have been the landless wage labourers. Employment
has become overwhelmingly (about three-quarters of the total)
temporary. The reception of income has become highly irregu-
lar, which has encouraged higher labour market participation, in
particular by women. The minimum wage has experienced
sharp fluctuations, and substantial deterioration in the late
1980s. More than half of the workers in modern firms are not

covered by social security. Housing conditions in rural areas are deplorable. Possibly the most important reason behind this deterioration in living conditions has to do with the restrictions and limitations imposed upon trade union activity and other forms of collective organisation of wage earners and the rural poor in general.

1.3 SOME GLOBAL EFFECTS OF THE MODEL

Changes such as the concentration of productive resources, output and exports, the increases in regional differences, the demographic shifts, and the evolution in the social class pyramid, should all be considered as structural rather than short term. They were provoked by the Pinochet regime policies, but no policy modification under democratic rule in the 1990s is likely to be able to reverse them. On the other hand, our argument is not that all these changes were necessarily bad.

The most notorious examples of land concentration are to be found in the forestry regions. Five conglomerates own more than half the total of plantations. Five exporters accounted for three-quarters of the sector's exports in 1987. There is not much concentration in fruit production, and some in fruit exports, but not as much as in forestry: 12 fruit firms export three-quarters of the total, with at least three among them being transnationals. Differences between geographical regions have become profound, qualitative rather than quantitative, and they appear in both the productive and the social spheres, in the respective degrees of market dynamism and in the patterns of population change and migration. The previous identity between the home space and the work space, typical of tenancy and sharecropping during the *hacienda* period, has been destroyed. Employment is now temporary rather than permanent. Housing, when available, is not on a rural plot any longer, but in cities, towns, villages and shanty towns.

Differentiation and increasing heterogeneity have affected everybody: peasants, landless rural labourers, and the rural bourgeoisie. But it would be wrong to assume that a massive process of proletarianisation has tended to eliminate the peasantry. Far from it, only 2 groups of peasants have lost their lands on a large scale: first, many among those benefited by land distribution after the processes of agrarian reform and counter-reform (the *parceleros*), and second, traditional peasants in for-estry areas. By contrast, in other regions some peasants have become part of the small rural bourgeoisie; they regularly hire labour and are engaged in capital accumulation on a small scale. In recent years there has been a large expansion in trade union activity. Rural society has become more and more complex, and the interests of different groups and the sources of conflict be-tween groups, increasingly more difficult to identify (let alone find ways to ameliorate conditions).

1.4 AGRICULTURE AND DEMOCRATISATION

A review of the information available suggests that the neo-liberal experience has generated a highly heterogeneous pattern of growth in agriculture. The Pinochet government's attitude of non-intervention (which was anyway always rather selective) has favoured the large conglomerates and those entrepreneurs with either unlimited access to capital or the best management abilities. In this way the neo-liberal policies have made possible a process of modernisation and accumulation which has been concentrated only in commercial agriculture – and, for that matter, in only a part of it. The military regime's attitude of refusing to interfere with the operation of markets has generated processes of differentiation among commercial agricultural en-terprises, among peasants, and among regions. To a large extent it has been wage earners who have paid the cost of this *'mod-ernización excluyente'*.

Whereas the main successes have been translated into mod-ernisation and foreign exchange earnings, there are at least four outstanding problems. The first has to do with the uncertainty of prospects, given that agrarian expansion relies heavily upon policies and decisions taken abroad. There are doubts as to the future stability of prices and markets, especially in the case of fruit (and Chilean fruit in particular). Producers and exporters have been unable to create mechanisms of coordination which would allow them to face the complex questions of marketing abroad in a more effective manner, something which actually has been attempted successfully by producers in other countries.

The second problem, which comes from outside the agricultural sector, refers to the limited possibilities for increasing the domestic demand for basic foodstuffs. This results from the depressed levels of real earnings, which have persisted for a long time.

The third problem is the marginalisation of the peasantry from the process of modernisation. This has to do with, among other things, difficulty in access to credit, absence of government support, and problems of access to markets. Increases in peasant yields have been less than satisfactory, which makes the peasant subsector appear a deadweight when compared with the agricultural sector as a whole. Many peasants have also shown a remarkable tendency to keep their lands despite all the obstacles; for all its merits, their refusal to sell means that a large share of the country's land resources are being used less than optimally.

Another weakness is the rather short-term horizons of entrepreneurs, especially the successful ones, who have devoted little of their profits to improving the working and living conditions of their personnel. This raises a serious question about the possibility of long-term survival of the neo-liberal model under political conditions different from those in force during the 1980s. In this connection there are two aspects to consider. One is that the presence of a hypothetical future increase in the demand for labour in urban areas, together with the low wages paid in the countryside and the lack of opportunities for the young, may contribute to generating a renewed wave of rural-urban migration, which itself may eventually represent a serious problem during the harvest period for the collection and packing of fruit for export markets. The second aspect is the possibility of labour conflicts. So far they have not been serious, but eventually they may acquire an explosive nature as workers become used to the new freedoms of the 1990s, and the honeymoon period between the population and the Aylwin government elapses. The leaderships of employers' associations are aware of this danger and have admitted it openly, but so far little notice has been taken of their recommendations to their members to change their wage policies and personnel management styles.

The neo-liberal model has provoked distortions in many areas, which will be difficult to correct in the context of a coherent rural development strategy, which should itself be compatible with the further democratisation of society. Productive resources are, once again, highly concentrated in a minority who, thanks to their successes, have a much stronger capacity for negotiation than that shown by the traditional landowners at the start of the land reform period. Moreover, these resources are to some extent devoted to production for external markets. The high level of participation by transnational enterprises suggests that these powerful players intend to stay in Chile for a long time.

Facing this prospect of increased entrepreneurial power, there is a large mass of peasant producers and landless wage earners, who have legitimate aspirations to improve their living standards and to participate in decisionmaking.

There is no doubt that there is some room for the objectives of all (or at least most) of these actors to be achieved, fully or partially. But it is also true that there will be an inevitable gap between aspirations or expectations on the one hand, and fulfilment on the other, between the proposals for the future of agriculture and the actual reality. What will happen in practice will be favourably affected by the highly successful process of transition to democracy between the plebiscite in October 1988 and the access to office by Aylwin in March 1990. The future evolution of the situation will largely depend upon the balance of political forces, and the trajectory of political events, in the first few years after 1990.

However, there are questions that will be present almost regardless of the political scenario. One of them is food, which according to many observers should be granted the top priority. Higher levels of real earnings will be reflected in a higher demand for food. Any strategy aimed at meeting this increased demand should involve a larger role for peasant producers, who will be expected to increase their output both for self-consumption and for selling purposes. Some peasants may even make a substantial contribution to exports. But the task of incorporating the peasants will not be easy, and it will have to be assumed essentially by the state.

There is also consensus about the need to maintain and increase exports. The potential dynamism of further agricultural exports is not under discussion. But this will require solving some of the problems mentioned above, together with some planning of future growth and the adequate coordination of marketing efforts.

At the time of writing there is no such thing as a peasant demand for land which is expressed in terms of massive action, demonstration or invasion. But possibly this will tend to appear (nobody knows with what level of strength), as peasants reconstruct their organisations and make their demands explicit. There are many regions from where dynamic activity is almost completely absent, and where labour demand is small. This means that improvement in living conditions depends almost entirely upon the amount of land and capital resources available to individual peasant families. Difficult decisions will have to be taken, since a balance will need to be found between justice for those who have little, and the possible trauma to be inflicted upon the owner classes by the threat to cherished property rights.

The economic problem of equity in the distribution of land will be compounded by the question of the political power which is always associated with the concentration of resources. Inevitably this question must be addressed, if relationships in rural society are to be redemocratised at all. The present situation is one in which certain regions are dominated by one single giant firm, which owns thousands of hectares and controls a large share of the local agro-industry (this is typically the case of forestry). Under these conditions it is not possible to implement development programmes addressed to individual entrepreneurs, peasants or wage earners. The concept of 'local development' itself becomes inapplicable. Regardless of the policies being attempted, in the final analysis it will be the all-powerful giant firm which will determine many aspects of the everyday and working lives of most local people.

To some extent, the expansion of agriculture in the 1980s rested upon cheap seasonal labour, but this situation is unlikely to persist if the workers are allowed to express their demands freely. The same is true of the low quality, or complete absence, of social services, which were passively accepted by the rural poor. This made it possible for the Pinochet government to allocate resources, in the most peaceful and unobtrusive manner, towards objectives which clearly did not favour the poor. But how can demands be constrained in an environment of higher participation?

The future of agriculture will be marked by the fact that it will be difficult to reconcile many different targets, some of them related to growth, others to equity. Possibly the most important objective should be the stability of the process of democratisation, which is likely to require a significant redistribution of income and wealth towards the poor in both urban and rural areas. Emphasis on agricultural production, important as it is, should be subjected to fulfilling stability and redistribution aims.

Two things may help to reduce the competition and antagonism which will inevitably appear. The first is the need for each social group to know clearly what its rights and duties are, in relation to society and to the state. These norms have never been clear in Chile. They were not there, for employers or employees, during the land reform process, and certainly they have not been present for the subordinate sectors under the military regime.

A second central factor refers to the need for participation by all sectors, both in the design of the policies which will affect them, and in organisations and associations of an economic, labour, and political character, locally, regionally, and nationally. This should make possible a legitimate channelling of demands, and it should contribute to making the business of government more transparent. A great discussion should be opened, at every level of society, about what we as Chileans have, what we want, and what we can do. Such a discussion of assets, aspirations and possibilities is indispensable in the case of rural society.

An important role should be played by local government, which ought to be concerned not only with the provision of services, but also with the development of a long-term vision which considers both problems and proposals.

To summarise, the neo-liberal model left as its inheritance some serious agrarian problems, not many resources to be devoted to their solution, and a long list of social conflicts which will be difficult to address in a context of compatibility between growth and distribution. Ideally, we should adopt an option which takes us away from ideologies and textbook paradigms and closer to the real creativity and needs of the nation.

2 The Agrarian Policy of the Aylwin Government: Continuity or Change?[1]

Cristóbal Kay

The key issue which I shall pursue in this chapter is the extent to which the agrarian policy being implemented during the current process of democratic transition in Chile represents a continuity or a change from the agrarian policy followed by the former authoritarian regime. Has there been a break with the neo-liberal economic model? It is well known that during the years of the dictatorship rural poverty has substantially increased and that agrarian development was highly uneven.[2] This leads me to explore the question of the extent to which the Aylwin government is willing and able to tackle the problems of rural poverty and unequal development in the countryside.

The short answer to these questions is that basically continuity (*continuismo*) predominates in the agrarian *economic* policy of the Aylwin government. However, new elements have also been introduced into this continuity which transform it into a 'neo-liberal model with a human face'. This 'human face' arises from the democratic opening of the political system and the attempts of the government to ameliorate the twin problems of poverty and uneven development. Is such an enhanced continuity desirable, and will it succeed in stimulating growth, reducing poverty, and democratising the political system?

2.1 STRUCTURAL CHANGES OF THE PINOCHET ERA: AGRICULTURE AS THE EPITOME OF MODERNITY

Before examining the agrarian policy of the Aylwin government it is useful to provide a context by highlighting the main structural transformations of the agrarian sector during the Pinochet period.[3] The most striking transformation is that today

19

agriculture embodies modernity, progress, and capitalist entrepreneurship while before it represented tradition, backwardness, semi-feudalism, and paternalism.[4] Today many observers characterise the agrarian sector as being in the grip of a modernising fever (*'un afán de modernización enfermizo'*) and some even argue that agriculture's dynamism is excessive, thereby creating new problems such as overproduction of fruits for export, ecological degradation, and alienation among the uprooted peasantry.

Since the rectification of the agrarian policy in 1983 agriculture has achieved an unusual dynamism, roughly trebling the long-run average yearly rate of growth between 1984 and 1988 (Echeñique, 1990). However, growth has been faltering in the last couple of years. This rectification reduced some of the unfair foreign competition facing domestic producers and provided some state support to farmers. Much of this growth was due to major increases in yields which reached levels amongst the highest in the developing world (Echeñique, 1990; Hojman, 1990a). Agriculture also attained the lowest sectoral rate of unemployment. It is important to bear in mind that this modernisation has its origins in the past (largely the years 1964–73) and that a high price was paid for it during the years 1974–83. The Aylwin government wants to build on this achievement, while at the same time seeking to ameliorate some of the costs and spreading the benefits more widely.

The structural transformations of the Pinochet period are now briefly analysed under the headings of agrarian counter-reform, modernisation and export boom.

Agrarian counter-reform

First and foremost, the termination of the agrarian reform through a process of counter-reform, which radically transformed the land tenure structure, needs to be highlighted.[5] The three most noteworthy aspects of this transformation are the final liquidation of the *hacienda* system, the consolidation of an agrarian bourgeoisie, and the formation of a sector of *parceleros*.

The changes in the land tenure structure can be seen in Table 2.1. Comparing the years 1965 and 1986 the 5–20 'basic irrigated hectares' (b.i.h.) farm sector more than doubled the percentage of land it owned while the over 80 b.i.h. farm sector was reduced by more than half. This is explained by the process

Table 2.1   Land distribution of farms, by size categories, 1965–86[a]

Size categories	1965	1972	1976	1979	1986
Below 5 b.i.h.*	9.7	9.7	9.7	13.3	14.0
5–20 b.i.h.*	12.7	13.0	37.2	29.0	26.0
20–80 b.i.h.*	22.5	38.9	22.3	36.3	31.0
Over 80 b.i.h.*	55.3	2.9	24.7	16.9	26.0
Other public agencies	0.0	0.0	0.0	4.0	3.0
Reform sector	0.0	35.5	9.5	0.0	0.0
Total[b]	100.2	99.8	103.4	99.5	100.0

Notes:
* b.i.h. stands for 'basic irrigated hectares'. The land area or physical hectares of a farm are expressed in basic irrigated hectares to ensure that farm size is measured in units of equivalent productive capacity.
1 b.i.h. is the equivalent of 1 hectare of prime irrigated land in the central Maipo River valley.
[a] Distributions are expressed as percentages.
[b] Columns may not sum to 100 due to rounding errors. However, there is a non-rounding error in 1976 which appears in the original.

Source: L. S. Jarvis, 'The unraveling of Chile's agrarian reform, 1973–1986', in W.C. Thiesenhusen (ed.), *Searching for Agrarian Reform in Latin America* (Boston: Unwin Hyman, 1989), p. 254.

of agrarian reform and counter-reform which resulted in the creation of a class of *parceleros* as well as of a class of medium-to-large capitalist farmers. On the one hand, many former landlords were able to retain or regain a part of their estate, called the *reserva*, which could not exceed 80 b.i.h. and was often considerably smaller. On the other hand, the remainder of the estate was subdivided into family farms of about 10 b.i.h. in size on average which were called *parcelas*.

The parcelation of the reformed sector has thus led to the growth in the 5–20 b.i.h. farm sector while the formation of *reservas* and the restoration of expropriated estates to former landlords during the counter-reform explains the growth of the 20–80 b.i.h. and over 80 b.i.h. farm size categories respectively (in the latter case after 1973). However, the farms of over 80 b.i.h. have today little in common with the former *hacienda*. The average farm size in this sector is far smaller than before being reduced from about 235 to about 125 b.i.h. (Jarvis, 1989, p. 257). More importantly, the social and technical relations of production have been completely transformed, as will now be discussed.

Modernisation

Second, the modernisation and capitalist transformation of the agrarian sector has been remarkable. The neo-liberal stress of the 'Chicago Boys' on the comparative advantage of Chilean agriculture gave a major impetus to agricultural and forestry exports, as well as forcing the pace of agricultural modernisation through international competition. In seeking to maximise profits and remain competitive farmers shifted to fruit and forestry export production wherever possible, raised yields through the use of modern inputs, increasingly mechanised farm activities, and capitalised their farms. This transformation was far from being smooth, and it was only with the rectification of 1983 that the problem of food security and modernisation of the commercial crop producing sector began to be tackled.

The intensified capitalist transformation of the medium-to-large farm sector (largely those farms above 40 b.i.h.) resulted in major changes in the social relations of production. The former tenants (*inquilinos* and *medieros*) were expelled and partly replaced with, or transformed into, temporary wage labourers (Cruz, 1986). The sex composition of seasonal workers also changed as a greater proportion of them became female, a process which has been referred to as 'the feminisation of temporary work' (Valdés, 1988). Furthermore, the farms were heavily capitalised, greatly increasing their capital–land ratio through mechanisation, agro-industrial development, and other investment. Often even the former houses of the tenants were demolished, as if to prevent the tenants' return, for they had been a major force behind the land reform. The capitalist farms have thus been cleansed of their resident population.

This massive expulsion and uprooting of the tenants has led to *desarraigo*, marginalisation, and the formation of rural shanty towns or *villorrios rurales* (Rivera and Cruz, 1984; Derksen, 1990). A whole peasant culture has been destroyed with it as the former tenants underwent a process of depeasantization (*descampesinización*). However, this change also affords new opportunities in the sense that the old ties of dependence, subordination, domination, patronage and clientelism have vanished. The social relations in the countryside are today no longer dependent on the former landlords but form part of the wider social system.

The centuries-old *hacienda* system has finally vanished from the Chilean countryside as a consequence of its capitalist transformation, the agrarian reform and counter-reform. On the one hand, the *hacienda* enterprise or central enterprise (the former demesne) has been completely separated from the tenant or decentralised enterprises (the 'internal peasantries') through the parcelation process.[6] On the other hand, the majority of the tenants have largely been proletarianised in a process which started many decades ago.[7]

The complex web of economic, social, political, cultural, and personal relationships which had been developing since the colonial period between landlords and peasants is thus no more (Kay, 1980). The *hacienda* enterprise has become a capitalist farm operated with only a fraction of the former labour force and mainly with temporary non-resident wage labour. Some of the former tenants have become *parceleros* while the majority have lost their access to land. A lucky few have experienced a process of peasantisation as their new *parcelas* are far larger than their former tenancies; but the majority of tenants have become proletarians or subproletarians seeking a living either in the rural or in the urban areas, and sometimes in both.[8]

The export boom

Last but not least, the drive into agricultural and forestry exports has been truly spectacular. From 1985 the agricultural foreign trade balance has consistently been positive, and this trend is very likely to continue having by now become firmly established. A major structural shift has thus occurred regarding agriculture's contribution to foreign exchange and position within the national economy. This is the first time since the mid-1930s that the agricultural sector has made a positive net contribution to foreign exchange: it is necessary to go back to the cereal export boom period of the 1850s–80s to find a comparable structural situation for the agricultural sector within the economy.

In recent years agricultural exports have been contributing about a fifth of total foreign exchange earnings as compared to about a fiftieth in the years before 1973 (Hojman, 1990a). The net contribution, of course, is less due to imports. But while agricultural imports before 1985 tended to exceed agricultural exports, agricultural exports have since then continued to grow fast while food imports have remained stable after their sharp decline in 1985 (Echeñique, 1990).

The rectification in agrarian policy during 1982–3, which resulted in the reintroduction of price bands for certain key crops, of higher tariffs for some food imports, and of purchasing powers, among other measures, has greatly stimulated internal food production to the extent that self-sufficiency has largely been achieved:[9] self-sufficiency in terms of the existing level and distribution of income which, of course, means that for many Chileans the levels of food consumption remain inadequate.

In short, the net foreign exchange contribution of the agricultural sector has today reached about 15 per cent of total export earnings.[10] This is above all the outcome of a major expansion and reorientation of agricultural production towards export markets, the seeds of which were sown during the 1960s with regards to forestry and fruit projects. But undoubtedly the new macroeconomic climate, the extremely high subsidies given to forestry plantations, and the newly released entrepreneurial energy and aggression have led to this major export drive which has to be credited to the Pinochet era. Those were years in which 'savage capitalism' ruled supreme, and whose savage edge the Aylwin government seeks to tame.

2.2 THE AGRARIAN POLICY OF THE AYLWIN GOVERNMENT: CONTINUITY WITH CHANGES OR A REALITY WHICH CANNOT BE IGNORED[11]

The context: 'Nadie Sabe Para Quién Trabaja'

Future historians analysing Chilean agrarian history in the twentieth century may well reach the conclusion that the essential historical break happened during the Christian Democrat government of 1964–70. This might appear as controversial to those who think that it was either the Allende government of 1970–3 or the Pinochet government of 1973–90 which marks an historical epoch. My argument is that the key agrarian transformation started with the land reform of the Frei government and that it was the Pinochet government which brought the land reform to a successful conclusion. To avoid misunderstandings, by 'successful conclusion' I mean from the point of view of the creation of an agrarian system which allowed the full development of capitalism. The economic policies of the Pinochet regime have led to the formation of an active land market, of a mobile and cheap rural labour force which has been freed from the means of production, and the development of a profit-seeking and modernising agrarian bourgeoisie. Furthermore, it is quite plausible to argue that the land tenure structure which exists today would not have differed fundamentally from that which was originally envisaged by the right-wing reformists within the Christian Democratic government.

The forces unleashed by Frei's agrarian policy could have been developed in either a capitalist or a socialist direction. When the capitalist forces within the Frei government and the Christian Democratic Party gained the upper hand the communitarian wing of the party broke away, formed their own political parties, which later joined the Allende government, and contributed to the socialist transformation in the countryside (Winn and Kay, 1974).[12] However, with the overthrow of the Popular Unity government the capitalist forces in Chilean society reasserted themselves again with a vengeance. Thus ultimately is has been the modernising capitalist forces, already encompassed in Frei's project, which have been able to flourish. The 'savage capitalism' of the Pinochet years, of course, made it possible greatly to accelerate the capitalist transformation in the Chilean countryside, as all social and political obstacles which could have slowed down or hindered such a process were violently removed. It is in this sense that Pinochet's policies brought to a logical and swift conclusion the structural changes and processes which the Frei government had unleashed, but developing them in a capitalist direction.

The three strategic elements in Frei's agrarian policy were land reform, peasant unionism (*sindicalización campesina*), and technological and economic modernisation (Kay, 1975, pp. 420–2). Except for the *sindicalización* all the other elements were also part and parcel of the Pinochet policy. During the Pinochet period the land reform was concluded and the modernisation was achieved in a dramatic and spectacular fashion. Rural trade unions were at first severely disarticulated, suffering the brunt of the repression in the countryside, but with the *Plan Laboral* (Labour Plan) a new legislative framework was created for the formation of trade unions. This new framework greatly fragmented and weakened trade union activity in the countryside (Silva, 1987, pp. 252–74). Nevertheless as compared to the pre-Frei years it still represented an advance, as hardly any trade unions then existed in the rural areas (Loveman, 1976).

Some key elements of Frei's agrarian policy were thus carried forward by Pinochet. For example, with regard to land reform the Pinochet government could have returned all the expropriated land to the former landlords, but it chose not to do so as the land reform also suited its objective of modernising Chilean agriculture. The repressive apparatus of the Pinochet dictatorship had also more to do with defeating the socialist challenge of the Allende years than with the modernisation of agriculture. Thus it would not be too far fetched to argue that in some respects the Pinochet regime represented a *continuismo* of the Frei period – minus, of course, the imposition of a dictatorship. This provocative statement might, in turn, explain Aylwin's continuity (plus democratisation, of course) rather than arguments about *leyes de amarre*,[13] not wanting to rock the boat, the need to overcome the shock and trauma of the past, seeking reconciliation, and so on. My argument is thus only apparently provocative as it can be used to legitimise Aylwin's continuity which can be interpreted as essentially a continuation of those elements of Pinochet's policies which originated during Frei's government.

Aylwin's agrarian policy: continuity with changes

When analysing the agrarian policy of the Aylwin government one is struck by the paucity of policy documents or declarations, and by the lack of any major policy initiatives regarding the agrarian sector. It is as if the election of a democratic government and securing its survival is considered as being its main achievement and objective. Undoubtedly the prime task of the Aylwin government should be to secure the redemocratisation of the country: the long period of the Pinochet dictatorship and the profound changes it created in the country is a reality which cannot be ignored. The socialist utopia is no more, and the progressive elements within Chilean society have lowered their horizons. Sustainable growth with equity and democratisation appears as a sufficient utopia in the post-Pinochet era.

In this process of *concertación*, of rebuilding civil society, and of finding a maximum of common agreement between former antagonistic social and political forces, the grand ideological fights and real confrontations between reformists and revolutionaries have gone. The new discourse is one of reconciliation, *reencuentro*, and *concertación*. The old discourse of the class struggle, of anti-imperialism, of revolution, and of socialism has vanished. It is thus not surprising to find that the Aylwin government has not launched any fundamental policy proposals so as not to resurrect the past and allow the opposition to revive the ghost of the Frei and Allende years. The Pinochet dictatorship has partly succeeded in rewriting history and changing people's perception, particularly of the Allende years which are likened to the incarnation of evil. This partly explains, but does not necessarily justify, the reluctance of the Aylwin government to open the land reform and trade unionisation issues, let alone the collectivisation and nationalisation theme.

I am not necessarily saying that the big issues of the 1960s and the early 1970s are still relevant today, but I am concerned that many of them remain taboo or marginalised in today's political discourse, and particularly in the media. The democratisation process will therefore need to have as one of its tasks to set the historical record straight by encouraging a more open debate of the past and thereby contributing towards a clearer vision of the future.

I will now explain briefly what seem to me to be the main aspects of Aylwin's agrarian policy. Not all of these policy issues are made explicit by the government.[14]

First, the government is fully committed to a social market economy. Full guarantees to, and respect of, private property rights and the capitalist system are assured. No new edition, reformulation, or revival of the land reform is contemplated, as this is considered a closed chapter. Foreign and domestic capital is not going to be expropriated. No state farms will be created although cooperative forms of organisation might be encouraged, particularly among smallholders, for credit, marketing, and technical assistance purposes. At present, no mention is made of recreating some of the state enterprises dealing with the agricultural sector which existed before their privatisation during the Pinochet regime.

Second, the agro-export model is to be continued. This requires a careful and stable management of foreign exchange policy so as to give the proper incentives to agro-exporters. It is thus likely that the exchange policy of recent years will not be altered. Special emphasis is to be given to forestry exports, with due regard to the ecological consequences, as this offers the greatest export potential. The foreign demand for Chilean fruit is reaching its limit as export markets are largely saturated;[15] it is thus necessary to find new types of exotic fruits which can be exported, to open up new export markets, to demand the removal of trading barriers by importing countries, and to move upmarket with better quality fruit.[16]

Third, the government will continue to provide technological support to farmers, but more emphasis will be given to the technological development of peasant farmers. It is planned to quadruple from 25 000 to 100 000 by 1994 the number of peasant farmers who will receive technical and other assistance from INDAP (Institute of Agrarian Development), either directly or through NGOs and private firms.[17] The government also intends to provide increased technical and credit support to peasant- and small-farmer cooperatives.

Fourth, the government aims to reduce rural poverty and provide better health, housing, education, and other social services to the rural areas. Part of the extra expenditure that this requires will be financed through increased taxation of the better-off farmers. Agricultural taxation will now be based on actual income (*renta efectiva*) rather than estimated income (*renta presunta*). As profits were usually underestimated, this change should raise more funds for the government.

Fifth, it is envisaged to continue and extend the price support policy and other promotional measures for crops destined for the domestic market. As import-substitution of foodstuffs has largely been achieved, it is necessary to raise the purchasing power of lower income groups so as to widen the internal market. This task is the more urgent given that poverty increased during the Pinochet era and that the *per capita* consumption levels of food are still well below the pre-1973 years.

Sixth, the government intends to reform the Plan Laboral. What might be required is to scrap Pinochet's Plan Laboral in its entirety, replacing it with a new labour code, but the Aylwin government is not as yet contemplating such action. The national peasant trade union organisation – the *Comisión Nacional Campesina* (CNC) – is certainly demanding that peasant unions should be allowed to be organised on a district level (*sindicatos comunales*) (at present, trade unions can be established only at enterprise level). The proposals of the CNC leave the choice open to the affiliates which at present they do not have (CNC, 1989; 1990; with regard to forestry workers, see CTF, 1990). Much concern has been expressed by government supporters about the lack of protective legislation for the seasonal workers (the *temporeros*) and about the need to organise them into unions which is hampered by the present legislation. To what extent the Aylwin government will be able to introduce new legislation to this effect remains to be seen. The aspiration of the CNC for the '*dignificación del trabajador agrícola*' (the dignification of the agricultural worker) is thus likely to reassert itself, and its achievement will depend greatly on the democratisation of social relations in the countryside.

Seventh, there is a great desire by the government to reform the town hall legislation and local government (*ley de municipios*).[18] The debate in Congress started in mid-1990 but has as yet (early 1991) not been concluded, given the misgivings and obstruction of the opposition. The reforms should ensure greater accountability of the mayors to their constituency as it is proposed that they should be elected rather than appointed by the President. This would also help to facilitate the provision of government services to the poorer sections of the community, and their social participation. Some of the mayors, which were all designated by Pinochet during his government, are boycotting the activities of the present government. It is expected that this reform should also benefit the rural population which was expelled from the estates and which has drifted during the last decade or so to villages and townships.

Eighth, the state apparatus is to be strengthened. The systematic dismantling of the state machinery through the privatisation of state enterprises, the drastic reduction in public employees, and so on, during the Pinochet years have greatly weakened the capacity of the state to intervene in the economy. The Aylwin government needs to expand the state sector so as to have a greater grip over economic developments and rectify the

limitations and inequalities of the free-market neoliberal economic system which was imposed by the 'Chicago Boys'.[19] This
has great relevance for the rural population and areas which
have been marginalised and excluded from the benefits of
growth and have borne the brunt of the costs of the repressive
modernisation process. The government does not intend to re-
create the size and even less the shortcomings of the old state
apparatus. On the contrary, it favours some decentralisation as
well as working through NGOs by subcontracting some activities to them. As many NGOs have been working with the poor
and in rural areas such a policy should benefit the rural poor.
However, the state apparatus inherited from Pinochet also has
many shortcomings which will require thorough reform, but it is
unclear to what extent Aylwin has the will and the power to
undertake such a necessary task.

Ninth, last but not least, the government intends to reduce the
high private debt of the agricultural sector. Many farmers borrowed too eagerly and too much, wanting to take full advantage
of the agro-export boom and to a lesser extent of the revived
internal market after the rectification of 1983. Many were caught
out by the fiasco of the 'poisoned grapes' which led to the
temporary collapse of Chile's largest fruit export market in the
USA during 1989. However, exporters of Chilean fruit were also
losing markets due to the poor quality of some shipments. Other
factors such as rising interest rates also contributed to the farmers' financial difficulties. However, the government is going to
focus its debt relief operations on the small farmers and let the
private banking and commercial sector take care of the remainder. But as the latter is going to happen in only a few instances it
is likely that some capitalist farmers and enterprises will face
bankruptcy. The government also intends to reduce and re-
schedule the land reform debt of the *parceleros*, thereby diminishing the chances of their proletarianisation.

To generalise, the agrarian policy of the Aylwin government
can be characterised as favouring redistribution with growth and
having a peasantist bias. It is envisaged that agricultural growth
rates might be slightly lower from those of the recent past, but it
is intended that they should be more sustainable socially and
ecologically. Priority is therefore to be given to diminishing the
acute inequalities by redirecting much of the government effort
in support of peasant agriculture and to those regions which, for

geographic and climatic reasons, were unable to join the export boom. The continuing revival of the domestic food market is thus particularly important as to reduce poverty and further stimulate production for the domestic market. Such a revival will, of course, greatly depend on macroeconomic policies and the overall performance of the economy.

2.3 THE PEASANT ECONOMY AND ITS REVITALISATION: A KEY PROBLEM

Chile is fortunate that its natural resources allow it potentially to expand simultaneously export and domestic production. Fruit and forestry exports have so far competed only to a minor extent with domestic food production over agricultural land. Future expansion of fruit and forestry plantations is unlikely to make major inroads into cropland due to the availability of surplus land, and climatic and other reasons. Competition for labour has also not yet been acute due to the existence of surplus labour largely generated by that labour reservoir which is the peasant family farm. The expulsion of labour from the capitalist farm sector has also contributed to swelling that labour surplus. However, labour might become increasingly a constraint in certain areas of high demand for seasonal labour; this is already happening in a few cases. But mechanisation, where possible, should help to relieve that constraint. The main competition is, of course, over capital. Thus the process of capital accumulation has to be sustained to ensure continued investment in both food and export activities; the continued flow of foreign capital has also to be welcomed, so long as it makes a positive contribution to the economy.[20]

This potential of Chilean agriculture should not blind us to the problems which this sector currently faces, or to those problems it will need to overcome in future to realise this potential. In what follows, I restrict myself to the main problem which Aylwin's government will encounter in implementing the core of its rural development strategy.

As a consequence of the agrarian reform and the parcelation of the reformed sector the peasant economy has acquired a new visibility, and its relative importance within the rural economy is increasingly being acknowledged. Previously the tenant enterprises within the *haciendas* (the internal peasant economies) were largely invisible, but when some of these tenants became *parceleros* (external peasant economies) their profile greatly increased. The fact that the *parceleros* are private owners of land and that they manage a substantially greater proportion of the land than previously, when they were dependent tenants, has naturally contributed to this greater presence and awareness of the peasant farm sector within agriculture and the national economy.

The relative importance of the peasant sector (mainly comprised of *minifundios* and *parcelas*), i.e. roughly the farms below 20 b.i.h. in size although not all of them, can be gauged from data presented earlier in Table 2.1 which show that it owned 40 per cent of the land in 1986. (The land is expressed in units of equal quality: the basic irrigated hectare – b.i.h.). A more recent and precise estimate calculates that in 1987 peasant producers controlled about 30 per cent of the land (Echeñique and Rolando, 1989, p. 27). The contribution of the peasant sector to agricultural output is about 25 per cent, which is below the percentage of land it owns as yields per hectare are lower in comparison with the capitalist farm sector (Echeñique and Rolando, 1989, p. 51). The peasant economy also produces mainly for the domestic market which has been less profitable than the export market. However, its contribution to employment is relatively more important, providing employment for about 38 per cent of the active agricultural labour force (Echeñique and Rolando, p. 24).

Thus a rural development strategy which seeks to develop the peasant producer sector is sensible, especially for reasons of equity, food security, employment and income distribution. Furthermore such a strategy is called for given the neglect, erosion and deterioration suffered by the peasant sector during the Pinochet government. Many peasants were expelled from the reform and capitalist farm sectors and many *parceleros* had to sell their land. Also a process of *minifundización*, or subdivision of *parcelas* among family members of *parceleros*, had set in. It is thus vital to support peasant agriculture so as to avoid its further decline and, above all, so as to reduce the growing technological gap between peasant and capitalist farming.

What is then the problem in implementing such a sensible rural development strategy? A peasantist programme requires for its success a lot of funding as well as consistency, continuity, perseverance and time to bear fruit: in short, such a programme is expensive and long term. This is where the key problem for the Aylwin government arises, as it has insufficient human and material resources at its disposal substantially to revitalise peasant farming and, in general, launch a full frontal assault on rural poverty. The *jibarización* or dismantling of the state and its reduction to a subsidiary role during the Pinochet era (Silva, 1990b) greatly hampers its ability to intervene in favour of the peasantry. Furthermore, the democratic government is under pressure to produce quick economic results. This may lead it to rely even more than it originally intended on the capitalist farmers for generating the increased agricultural output, and thus drive it to devote insufficient attention to the peasant sector.

Notes

1. The following persons have generously shared their ideas on Chilean agriculture with me: G. Arroyo, R. Baraona, J. Bengoa, T. Cox, M. E. Cruz, G. Falabella, S. Gómez, F. Lira, E. Mlynarz, J. Nagel, E. Ortega, R. Rivera, A. Schejtman, and O. Torres. I am especially grateful to P. Silva for commenting on an earlier draft of this chapter. They are, of course, not responsible for my particular views on Chilean agriculture nor for any errors and weaknesses this chapter may have. I am also grateful for the magnificent library support I received from Mariana Giacaman and the Grupo de Investigaciones Agrarias (GIA) of the Universidad Academia de Humanismo Cristiano. Many thanks also to the Grupo de Estudios Agrarios (GEA) of the same university for their invitation to attend their cycle of conferences on Chilean agriculture. Finally, my acknowledgment to the Institute of Social Studies (ISS) in The Hague for financing my research trip to Chile. A draft version of this chapter was presented at the conference on 'The Transition to Democracy in Chile' which was jointly organised by CERC of the Universidad Academia de Humanismo Cristiano, Santiago, St Anthony's College, Oxford, and the Institute of Latin American Studies of the University of Liverpool, held at Liverpool University in December 1990.
2. I have examined the repressive and distortionary nature of the military's agrarian policy in an earlier article, see Kay (1985).
3. The following publications provide useful overviews of agrarian change and policy during the Pinochet years: Jarvis (1985); Ortega (1987); Silva (1987); Cruz (1986); Gómez and Echeñique (1988); Jarvis (1989); Cox, Niño de Zepeda and Rojas (1990); Hojman (1990). For a valuable review essay of the key literature on this topic see Silva (1990a). From this list the book by Gómez and Echeñique was particularly influential in bringing

about the '*vuelco de los intelectuales*' ('the turn of the intellectuals'). The predominant view among left-wing thinkers on the agrarian changes brought about by the Pinochet government tended to be completely negative; the book by Gómez and Echeñique has the merit of highlighting both faces of the modernising process.

4. The drastic change in the agrarian system, which started with the land reform, together with the liberalisation of the economic system during the Pinochet years, have greatly increased the agricultural producers' awareness and ability to react to changes in prices as well as to other economic indicators. This high degree of price-responsiveness of today's producers is sometimes used to criticise structuralists who emphasised rigidities, inelasticities, and so on. However, such critiques are ahistorical and, in my view, it is perfectly possible to explain the new situation within the structuralist paradigm. For recent studies on agricultural price elasticities and supply responsiveness see Hojman (1990b), and Coeymans and Mundlak (1991). For an interesting debate on the relative importance of changes in the coherence of macroeconomic policy and in land tenure structure on aggregate agricultural supply response, which in some ways echoes the neoclassical – structuralist debate, see Quiroz, Barahona and Valdés (1988); Jarvis (1990); and the rejoinder by Barahona, Quiroz and Valdés (1990).

5. For a brief and helpful analysis of the privatisation of the reformed sector see Silva (1991). For the most comprehensive study on the counter-reform see Jarvis (1989).

6. For a discussion of concepts such as the *hacienda* system, *hacienda* enterprise, internal and external peasant economies in the Latin American context see Kay (1979).

7. For an historical analysis of the capitalist development of the *hacienda* system in Chile see Kay (1977), and for the history of the agrarian reform in Chile see Huerta (1989).

8. The book by Rodríguez and Venegas (1989) and the essay by Korovkin (1990) provide illuminating and detailed accounts of the process of peasant differentiation arising from the counter-reform in two particular areas of central Chile.

9. For a detailed description of the various rectification or adjustment policies see Sanfuentes (1987). For an analysis of the experience with agricultural price bands see Muchnik and Allue (1991).

10. For a comprehensive analysis and statistical study of the impact of trade liberalisation, exchange rate, and agricultural pricing policies on the performance of the agricultural sector and on agriculture's contribution to foreign exchange revenues see Valdés, Muchnik and Hurtado (1990).

11. For a competent overview of Aylwin's overall economic programme and the place of the agricultural sector within it, see Hojman (1990c). In a brief article Hojman (1990d) also stresses the continuity of Aylwin's agrarian policies with those of Pinochet after 1985.

12. The right-wing within the Christian Democratic Party and the Frei government favoured the parcelation of the reformed sector while the left-wing favoured communitarian property (i.e. producer cooperatives). The left-wing reformists within the Christian Democratic Party broke away from the party during the last two years or so of the Frei government

later joining the Popular Unity coalition of parties. This communitarian approach can be exemplified in the writings of, and government positions held by, Jacques Chonchol. He was in charge of INDAP (the government office concerned mainly with the development of the peasant sector) at the beginning of the Frei government. He resigned and was a key figure in one of the break-away groups from the Christian Democratic Party. He became Minister of Agriculture during the Allende government, providing a key link between the communitarian inspired Christian Democrat groups and the socialist groups at party and *campesino* levels. See Silva Solar and Chonchol (1965); Chonchol (1967) and (1972).

13. *Leyes de amarre* (laws which bind or tie you down) are the various laws which the Pinochet regime bequeathed to any future democratic government with the purpose of limiting the powers of such a government with regard to prosecuting those persons who violated human rights, to changing existing legislation, and to introducing new legislation which might facilitate its task of democratisation and of a creating a more equitable path of development.

14. I have used the following sources, among others, for gaining an insight into the agrarian programme of Aylwin's government and its background: Cox (1988); Unauthored (1989); Comisión Agraria de la Concertación (1989); Concertación de Partidos por la Democracia (1990); the first *Mensaje* (in which the government programme, implementation, achievements, and so on, are presented: a sort of state of the nation address) of President Aylwin delivered to parliament on 21 May 1990; various interviews given to the press by high officials from agrarian ministries or offices; and so on. However, the best source were the interviews I had with agrarian specialists and policymakers who, of course, bear no responsibility for the interpretation I have given to their thoughts. I have also used the cuttings of articles on agrarian issues from a variety of Chilean newspapers and magazines which are compiled periodically by the FAO regional office in Santiago. My thanks to the FAO for sending me these informative compilations which are entitled *Selección de Recortes de Noticias Aparecidas en los Diarios Chilenos*. Additionally I have made use of another collection of newspaper cuttings which I was able to consult in the library of the Grupo de Investigaciones Agrarias (GIA) in Santiago.

15. For recent studies on the forestry sector see Contreras (1988); Wisecarver (1988); and Morales (1989).

16. See the technically competent articles on this theme in *Panorama Económico de la Agricultura* which is a magazine published bimonthly by the Department of Agricultural Economics of the Faculty of Agriculture, Catholic University of Chile in Santiago. So far, Aylwin's government has been unable to persuade fruit exporters and opposition politicians to agree to joint private and state quality controls on fruit destined for the export market. The government's proposal was modest and sensible and very much in the interest of exporters but it was opposed for ideological reasons as it was seen as the thin edge of further state controls and activities in the countryside.

17. Information provided by Maximiliano Cox, Under-Secretary for Agriculture in the Aylwin government, in his talk given at the conference on

'Agrarian Reality in Today's Chile'. This conference was organised by the Grupo de Estudios Agrarios (GEA) of the Universidad Academia de Humanismo Cristiano and took place in Santiago on 28 August 1990.

18. For a discussion on the limitations, possibilities, and requirements for reform of the local government system with regard to the countryside in Chile see Ahumada *et al.* (1988).

19. For useful analyses of the neo-liberal economic model (also referred to as neo-conservative, radical conservative, and repressive or militant monetarism) and its performance during the Pinochet years see, among others, Foxley (1983), Ramos (1986), and Edwards and Edwards (1987).

20. The government intends to remove the high subsidy given to the large forestry conglomerates and to restrain their predatory urges, whatever their nationality. To what extent it will limit their oligopolistic powers and reduce their high degree of concentration remains to be seen.

References

Ahumada, J. *et al.* (1988) *Gobierno Local y Participación Social: Debate desde una Perspectiva Agraria* (Santiago: GIA).

Barahona, P., Quiroz, J. and Valdés, A. (1990) 'Respuesta al comentario del profesor Jarvis', *Cuadernos de Economía*, vol. 27, no. 80, pp. 115–17.

Chonchol, J. (1967) 'Proposiciones para una acción política en el período 1967–70 de una vía no capitalista de desarrollo', *Separata Especial de PEC*, no. 239.

Chonchol, J. (1972) 'La reforma agraria y la experiencia chilena', in CESO/CEREN, *Transición al Socialismo y Experiencia Chilena* (Santiago: PLA).

Coeymans, J. E. and Mundlak, Y. (1991) 'Aggregate agricultural supply response in Chile, 1962–82', *Food Policy*, vol. 16, no. 1, pp. 17–22.

Comisión Agraria de la Concertación (1989) *Propuesta Agraria. Avance de Documento de Síntesis* (Santiago) (mimeo).

Comisión Nacional Campesina (CNC) (1989) *Proyecto Democrático para el Desarrollo Rural del Movimiento Campesino Chileno* (Santiago: CNC).

Comisión Nacional Campesina (CNC) (1990) *Hacia la Dignificación del Campesinado Chileno* (Santiago: CNC).

Concertación de Partidos por la Democracia (1990) *Bases Programáticas del Gobierno de Reconstrucción Democrática* (Santiago) (mimeo).

Confederación Nacional de Trabajadores Forestales (CTF) (1990) *Propuesta Forestal y Laboral para la Democracia* (Concepción: CTF).

Contreras, R. (1988) *Más Allá del Bosque* (Santiago: Editorial Amerinda).

Cox, M. (1988) 'Bases de un programa para el desarrollo sostenido y equitativo del agro chileno (versión preliminar)', *Seminario Internacional La Agricultura Latinoamericana: Crisis, Transformaciones y Perspectivas*, Punta de Tralca, Chile (Santiago: GIA/CLACSO).

Cox, M., Niño de Zepeda, A. and Rojas A. (1990) *Política Agraria en Chile, Del Crecimiento Excluyente al Desarrollo Equitativo* (Santiago: CEDRA).

Cruz, M. E. (1986) 'De inquilinos a temporeros, de la hacienda al poblado rural', *Serie Documentos de Trabajo*, no. 21, Grupo de Investigaciones Agrarias (GIA), Universidad Academia de Humanismo Cristiano (Santiago).

Derksen, M. M. J. (1990) 'Santa Sabina: Surviving in a Rural Shanty Town', in Hojman (1990).

Díaz, H. P. (1990) 'Proletarianisation and marginality: the modernisation of Chilean agriculture', in Hojman (1990).

Echeñique, J. (1990) 'Las dos cara de la agricultura y las políticas posibles', *Proposiciones*, no. 18, pp. 145–58.

Echeñique, J. and Rolando, N. (1989) *La Pequeña Agricultura, Una Reserva de Potencialidades y una Deuda Social* (Santiago: Agraria).

Edwards, S. and Edwards, A. C. (1987) *Monetarism and Liberalization. The Chilean Experiment* (Cambridge, Mass.: Ballinger).

Falabella, G. (1990) 'Trabajo temporal y desorganización social', *Proposiciones*, no. 18, pp. 251–68.

Foxley, A. (1983) *Latin American Experiments in Neoconservative Economics* (Berkeley: University of California Press).

Gómez, S. and Echeñique, J. (1988) *La Agricultura Chilena: Las Dos Caras de la Modernización* (Santiago: FLACSO/Agraria).

Hojman, D. E. (1990a) 'Introduction', in Hojman (1990).

Hojman, D. E. (1990b) 'What makes Chilean agriculture tick? Estimation and interpretation of elasticities in representative markets', in Hojman (1990).

Hojman, D. E. (1990c) 'Chile after Pinochet: Aylwin's Christian Democrat economic policies for the 1990s', *Bulletin of Latin American Research*, vol. 9, no. 1 pp. 25–47.

Hojman, D. E. (1990d) 'Agricultura chilena y economía internacional: continuidad y cambio en la década de los 90', in Colloque International Université Toulouse-le-Mirail, *Agricultures et Paysanneries en Amérique Latine, Atelier V* (Toulouse: Université Toulouse-le-Mirail).

Hojman, D. E. (ed.) (1990) *Neo-liberal Agriculture in Rural Chile* (London: Macmillan).

Huerta, M. A. (1989) *Otro Agro para Chile. La Historia de la Reforma Agraria en el Proceso Social y Político* (Santiago: Ediciones Chile América CESOC).

Jarvis, L. S. (1985) *Chilean Agriculture under Military Rule. From Reform to Reaction. 1973–1980*, Research Series, no. 59 (Berkeley: Institute of International Studies, University of California).

Jarvis, L. S. (1989) 'The unraveling of Chile's agrarian reform, 1973–1986', in W. C. Thiesenhusen (ed.), *Searching for Agrarian Reform in Latin America* (Boston, Mass.: Unwin Hyman).

Jarvis, L. S. (1990) 'Reformas de las políticas económicas de la agricultura chilena y la respuesta de la oferta agregada: otro punto de vista', *Cuadernos de Economía*, vol. 27, no. 80, pp. 103–14.

Kay, C. (1975) 'Agrarian reform and the transition to socialism in Chile, 1970–1973', *The Journal of Peasant Studies*, vol. 2, no. 4, pp. 418–45.

Kay, C. (1977) 'The development of the Chilean *hacienda* system, 1850–1973', in K. Duncan and I. Rutledge (eds), *Land and Labour in Latin America. Essays on the Development of Agrarian Capitalism in the Nineteenth and Twentieth Centuries* (Cambridge: Cambridge University Press).

Kay, C. (1979) 'The hacienda system, proletarianization and agrarian reform: the roads of the landlord and of the subordinate peasant to capitalism', in Albuqurque, M. B. and Dias David, M. (eds), *El Sector Agrario en América Latina. Estructura Económica y Cambio Social* (Stockholm: Instituto de Estudios Latinoamericanos).

Kay, C. (1980) 'Transformaciones de las relaciones de dominación y dependencia entre terratenientes y campesinos en Chile', *Revista Mexicana de Sociología*, vol. 42, no. 2, pp. 751–97.

Kay, C. (1985) 'The monetarist experiment in the Chilean countryside', *Third World Quarterly*, vol. 7, no. 2, pp. 301–22.

Korovkin, T. (1990) 'Neo-liberal counter-reform: peasant differentiation and organisation in Tártaro, central Chile', in Hojman (1990).

Loveman, B. (1976) *Struggle in the Countryside. Politics and Rural Labor in Chile, 1919–1973* (Bloomington: Indiana University Press).

Morales, J. (1989) *El Desarrollo Forestal en Concepción* (Santiago: GEA).

Muchnik, E. and Allue, M. (1991) 'The Chilean experience with agricultural price bands', *Food Policy*, vol. 16, no. 1, pp. 67–73.

Ortega, E. (1987) *Transformaciones Agrarias y Campesinado. De la Participación a la Exclusión* (Santiago: CIEPLAN).

Quiroz, J., Barahona, P and Valdés, A. (1988) 'Reformas económicas en la agricultura y respuesta de la produccion agregada: Chile 1960–1987', *Cuadernos de Economía*, vol. 25, no. 76, pp. 391–403.

Ramos, J. (1986) *Neoconservative Economics in the Southern Cone of Latin America, 1973–1983* (Baltimore: The Johns Hopkins Press).

Rivera, R. and Cruz, M. E. (1984) *Pobladores Rurales. Cambios en el Poblamiento y el Empleo Rural en Chile* (Santiago: GIA).

Rodriguez, D. and Venegas, S. (1989) *De Praderas a Parronales. Un Estudio sobre Estructura Agraria y Mercado Laboral en el Valle de Aconcagua* (Santiago: GEA).

Sanfuentes, A. (1987) 'Chile: effects of the adjustment policies on the agriculture and forestry sector', *CEPAL Review*, no. 33, pp. 115–27.

Silva, P. (1987) *Estado, Neo-Liberalismo y Política Agraria en Chile, 1973–1981* (Amsterdam: CEDLA).

Silva, P. (1990a) 'Agrarian change under the chilean military government', *Latin American Research Review*, vol. 25, no. 1, pp. 193–205.

Silva, P. (1990b) 'State Subsidiarity in the Chilean Countryside', in Hojman (1990).

Silva, P. (1991) 'The military regime and restructuring of land tenure', *Latin American Perspectives*, vol. 18, no. 1, pp. 15–32.

Silva Solar, J. and Chonchol, J. (1965) *El Desarrollo de la Nueva Sociedad en América Latina. Hacia un Mundo Comunitario* (Santiago: Editorial Universitaria).

Unauthored (1989) *Propuesta. Políticas y Programas Agro Rurales para el Gobierno Democrático de la Concertación* (Santiago, 1 September 1989) (mimeo).

Valdés, A., Muchnik, E. and Hurtado, H. (1990) *Trade, Exchange Rate, and Agricultural Pricing Policies in Chile*, 2 vols., World Bank Comparative Studies, The Political Economy of Agricultural Pricing Policy (Washington, D.C.: World Bank).

Valdés, X. (1988) 'Feminización del mercado de trabajo agrícola: las temporeras', in Centro de Estudios de la Mujer, *Mundo de Mujer: Continuidad y Cambio* (Santiago: Ediciones CEM).

Winn, P. and Kay, C. (1974) 'Agrarian reform and rural revolution in Allende's Chile', *Journal of Latin American Studies*, vol. 6, no. 1, pp. 135–59.

Wisecarver, D. (1988) 'El sector forestal chileno: políticas, desarrollo del recurso y exportaciones', *Documento de Trabajo*, no. 112 (Santiago: Instituto de Economía, Universidad Católica de Chile).

3 Agriculture and Forestry: Reflections on Liberal Policies

Shanti P. Chakravarty[1]

3.1 INTRODUCTION

The intellectual basis for development planning has come under attack of late. It is alleged that developing countries which favoured import-substitution policies fared worse than those which adopted more outward-looking economic policies. The latter group of countries directed resources towards sectors in which they had comparative advantage, or to sectors in which they could develop comparative advantage (Little, 1982). One consequence of this line of reasoning is that decisions about agriculture are increasingly being taken on the same economic criteria as those applied to industry. For example, production of cash crops for export in preference to either the growing of food for domestic consumption or the fabrication of goods for import substitution is being encouraged if the added value, computed in international prices, of the first activity is greater. Forestry projects are being allowed in the private sector which might have been shunned in the past. Even if the case for market-determined economic priorities is accepted, there are problems about deciding how to react to market signals, especially in the presence of uncertainty concerning prices. There is also no unique market-determined way of responding to environmental problems which arise in the course of economic activity. We examine two issues with reference to recent developments in Chile. First, is the declining reliance on copper exports in favour of increasing dependence on the earnings from the export of agricultural products likely to expose Chile to greater volatility in her balance of trade? We then consider, after establishing a rationale for that concern, whether the market-based policies in forestry can address the question of inter-generational equity.

A central plank of the debate concerns the extent to which

markets can be relied upon to provide the information needed for pursuing even those goals which are set by the markets themselves (Ackerlof, 1970). Even if information were disseminated by the markets, is there a unique set of response that is likely to be observed from market participants (Tversky and Kahneman, 1981)? These arguments are not explicitly addressed in this chapter; instead, a related set of questions is examined.

Often disputes between the proponents of different views on development can be traced to assumptions which are amenable to empirical scrutiny. For example, pleas for self-sufficiency in food production are often inspired by the fear of price fluctuations in agriculture, and a desire to follow the especially risk-averse maximin strategy, explained below, in the face of uncertainty. Concerns about market-led developments in natural resource exploitation reduce to the question of how to determine the appropriate discount rate in cost–benefit analysis, to balance the competing claims between generations.

Does the adherence to market principles necessarily entail the development of export agriculture? Do price fluctuations render trade in agriculture less attractive than trade in other commodities? Price fluctuations would introduce market inefficiency if there were credit rationing, or if the efficient functioning of the insurance market was impeded due to paucity of information on which to judge future trends. Price fluctuations might also make trade inadvisable if the especially conservative maximin criterion was adopted for decisions under uncertainty. An additional question arises in considering those aspects of agriculture – for example, forestry – which have consequences for the quality of the environment. Are investments in the exploitation of forestry resources to earn foreign exchange consistent with responsibility for protecting environmental resources for future generations? What is it that is owed to these generations?

If a country enjoys comparative advantage in the production of certain goods, adherents of market economics would argue that the country should concentrate its efforts on producing those goods. Anything else that is needed could then be imported from the proceeds earned by exporting some of the first set of goods; the standard of living in the country should thus be higher than it would otherwise be, under the alternative policy of self-sufficiency. This conclusion needs to be elaborated on two grounds. The first concerns criteria for judging comparative advantage in the presence of uncertainty. The second concerns the criteria for project selection in the context of possible divergence between the market-determined and the socially-optimum rates of exploitation of natural resources, when the effect of such activity on future generations is taken into account. We highlight some of the points that need to be taken on board in analysing both these points.

3.2   THE ISSUES

Price fluctuations

Even amongst industrialised countries in the West which publicly adhere to market principles in the formulation of economic policy, there is a view held in influential circles in government that the activity of food production must be treated as an exception. This view that agriculture must have a special place in the scheme of economic organisation, sheltered from the vagaries of the market, also prevails in many developing countries. Two fears, about sovereignty and about instability of the international price of agricultural products, underlie this approach. The first concerns the protection of foreign policy objectives against external pressure, based on the assumption that dependence on food imports could cause greater erosion of sovereignty than dependence on most other kinds of imports. It is assumed that a country dependent on the import of staples might have to concede some cherished principles of foreign policy to be able to raise finance to make up the shortfall in international markets. There are also other fears – for example, about food security in wartime – which have been raised in support of the so-called national security argument for agricultural subsidy (Winters, 1988, section VI). Whilst the above concerns are 'non-economic', there is another seemingly 'non-economic' criterion that is amenable to economic analysis. This objective is based on the fear of domestic upheavals caused by fluctuating food prices. 'Safe, secure, stable and sufficient food supplies' are cited as objectives of agricultural policy in a range of OECD countries, including the whole of the European Community, Japan, Canada, Austria, New Zealand, Switzerland, Finland, Iceland, Norway and Sweden (see Winters, 1988, Table 1). It is this second aspect of the tendency towards shielding agriculture from the market that is of special interest to economists.

Commodity-exporting developing nations have experienced wide fluctuations in their terms of trade, there having been long periods of decline, and many of them are wary of dependence on food imports. Citing evidence presented in Helleiner (1986), Sarris (1988, p. 33) argues that 'the main desire of low income African countries has been to stabilize import volume more than to increase export earnings . . . the desire for food security tended to favour a production structure more influenced by variability than by static average profitability criteria'. This desire is not confined to the lower income group amongst African countries. The domestic political upheavals occasioned by food price rises are observed also elsewhere. Twice in the 1980s, agitation against the Polish government was triggered by rises in food prices.

The tendency to shun agricultural trade has two facets; the first is a desire for self-sufficiency in staples and the second is a suspicion of the proposition that cash crops are no worse than other products which could be developed as foreign currency earners. Insofar as Chile has not become more dependent on agricultural import, but has instead become more dependent on the earnings from agricultural export, it is the logic of the second aspect of the above tendency which is examined below.

We consider recent developments in Chilean agriculture which, at first sight, appear to run counter to the perceived fears just considered. Chile invested heavily in export agriculture in the 1980s for earning foreign exchange.

Forestry

Many developing countries depend on fuelwood as a major source of energy. Wood stocks are being depleted at an alarming rate (Anderson and Fishwick, 1984). Harvesting exceeds sustainable yields by more than 100 per cent in many countries even outside of the African continent. Now these forestry resources are in danger of being further eroded due to pressures to earn foreign exchange to service international debts.

The forest area of the world has continued to shrink. This has adverse effects on soil quality and air pollution. The environmental damage through loss of forests in the Federal Republic of

Germany between 1983 and 1985 has been estimated at DM
2.3–2.9 billion (Pearce, *et al*, 1989, p. 58). If the loss of recreational values is taken into account, this estimate is more
than doubled.

There is an opinion that renewable resource depletion should
be confined to the rate circumscribed by the requirements of sustainable yield. 'Sustainable yield' in the above context is defined as
the annual increase in the forestry stock; the stock would thus be
sustained only if the annual rate of tree felling could be limited to
the annual rate of regeneration. An exclusively market-determined
rate of depletion might fail to satisfy the sustainability requirement. We now examine this argument, and also reflect on the
rationale for sustainability, and then consider the issues which
have to be taken on board for evaluating forestry projects.

3.3 CHILEAN AGRICULTURE

The structure of the Chilean economy has changed considerably
over the 1980s. One of the more remarkable changes is the
lessening of dependence on copper exports in favour of exports of
non-traditional items in agriculture; this export industry has
developed partly because of the availability of cheap female
labour. The main thrust of recent economic policy has been to
take comparative cost advantage as the criterion for selecting
export industries.

From published data, it can be inferred that wages in mining
and manufacturing have increased at a faster rate than those in
agriculture. This inference is based on the observation that the
wages of unskilled workers in urban areas have risen slower than
those in mining and also in manufacturing. Unskilled workers'
wages have not even kept pace with increases in the consumer
price index (see Table 3.1).

Whilst it appears from Table 3.2 that the share of agriculture
in the Gross Domestic Product of Chile has slightly declined,
from 9.2 to 9.0 per cent between 1983 and 1989, the rate of
growth in the output of agriculture during the later years of this
period has been faster, as demonstrated in Table 3.3.

What is even more remarkable about developments in Chilean
agriculture is its growing role as an export earner. Between 1981
and 1988, Chilean export earnings almost doubled, registering

Table 3.1   Trends in wages and salaries index, December 1982 = 100

| | National wages and salaries | | | Urban wages (unskilled) | |
Year	CPI	Mining	Manufacturing	Services	Other
1984	134.2	139.4	128.7	126.7	124.86
1986	209.6	219.4	196.4	180.2	181.07
1988	288.1	314.2	288.0	260.94	263.5
1990 (Feb.)	383.7	421.0	403.1	355.0	372.3

Source: Calculated from data published in Banco Central de Chile, *Boletín Mensual*.

Table 3.2   Composition of the Gross Domestic Product, Billions 1977 pesos

Year	Agriculture	Manufacturing	Construction	Mining	GDP
1983	30.02	65.47	17.02	29.11	327.18
1986	37.11	82.80	20.85	31.52	376.63
1989	42.32	98.98	27.56	35.63	470.24

Source: Banco Central de Chile, *Boletín Mensual*. The figures for agriculture include livestock, forestry and fishing.

Table 3.3   Growth rates in real production at market prices

Year	Agriculture	Manufacturing	Construction	Mining	GDP
1982	−1.2	−21.0	−23.8	−5.7	−14.1
1983	−2.5	3.1	−5.0	−1.9	−0.7
1984	7.5	9.8	4.2	4.4	6.3
1985	5.6	1.2	16.1	2.2	2.4
1986	8.8	8.0	1.3	1.4	5.5
1989	10.7	10.0	12.7	8.4	10.0

Source: *Economic and Social Progress in Latin America*, 1987 Report, and Banco Central de Chile, *Boletín Mensual*. The figures for Agriculture include livestock, forestry and fishing.

an increase of 84 per cent (Table 3.4). Earnings from agricultural exports, however, more than doubled, rising by 158 per cent. Some of the figures are even more impressive if the agricultural exports are broken down into components, as is done in Table 3.5. Export earnings from fishing and other agricultural pro-

Table 3.4   Commodity composition of exports

Year	Agriculture	Mining	Manuf.	Total	Agriculture	Mining	Manuf.
	Exports (fob, $m)				Share of total exports (%)		
1971	29.4	813.2	119.6	962.2	3.1	84.5	12.4
1981	365.4	2177.5	1293.6	3836.5	9.5	56.8	33.7
1986	683.0	2096.1	1419.7	4198.8	16.3	49.9	33.8
1988	930.4	3848.3	2273.1	7051.8	13.2	54.6	32.2

Source: Banco Central de Chile, *Boletín Mensual*.

Table 3.5   Composition of agricultural exports, US$ million

Year	Livestock	Forestry	Fishing	Other	Total
1981	29.1	2.1	66.2	171.6	268.0
1986	39.4	1.7	78.9	443.0	563.0
1988	58.0	2.6	178.6	452.0	691.2

Source: Banco Central de Chile, *Boletín Mensual*.

ducts, especially fruits, rose by 170 and 163 per cent, respectively.

Another point to note is that the development of export crops was not at the expense of production for domestic consumption. Food imports did not rise during the period in question. Imports for consumption of agricultural goods in 1981 stood at US$ 32.9 million. The figure had halved by 1987, when it stood at US$ 13.0 million. Intermediate imports for agricultural production also declined. The figure stood at US$ 327 million in 1981, but it was only US$ 83.9 million in 1987 (*Boletín Mensual*). Whilst the area devoted to the production of cereals declined in the latter half of the 1980s, production increased due to better yields.

The food security argument against getting involved in agricultural trade thus appears not to have been challenged by the government. Domestic agriculture continued to receive some subsidy, shielded from the market, but market arguments of comparative advantage informed the choice of agriculture for export, as evidenced by the greater emphasis on export agriculture. For example, irrigation works have been financed out of Exchequer funds, and government intervenes in the markets to maintain a floor on the prices or certain agricultural products (Hojman 1990: 1992). The question which needs to be examined

Table 3.6   Agricultural area and production

Year	Cereals	Legumes/Potatoes	Industrial crops	Fruits
1983–4	781(21.2)	212(11.6)	57(22.1)	80.7(990.3)
1984–5	801(23.6)	200(10.5)	83(21.9)	88.0(1067.5)
1985–6	798(26.8)	201(9.2)	138(27.9)	96.6(1238.6)
1986–7	875(28.2)	211(8.5)	120(27.8)	105.2(1388.4)
1987–8	793(28.0)	191(10.6)	130(26.6)	115.1(1558.9)

Note: Area is measured in thousands of hectares and production, shown in brackets, is measured in millions of metric quintals for products other than fruits. Fruit output is measured in thousands of tons. The figures for area devoted to fruit production, but not the quantity of output, relate to calendar years.

Source: Calculated from data in *Boletín Mensual*.

is the following. In the presence of market imperfections in international lending, did it make sense to develop export agriculture? Due to these imperfections, which arise because the price of loans (the interest rate) is not determined by risk-adjusted potential return from lending, it is not possible to insure against large fluctuations in earnings. Information needed to calculate the levels of risk and return is lacking. Instead of an efficient clearing market, we observe that international lending is characterised by credit rationing. A problem for Chile in following market signals for the selection of goods for export was thus that of the greater need for ensuring stability of foreign currency earnings, in preference to greater average export earnings. The country had to run surpluses in merchandise trade to be able to service its foreign debts. Due to credit rationing, new money was not readily available to tide over difficulties. Big gyrations in the trade surplus would have caused further problems, even if the average value of that surplus were to show improvements. In the context of credit rationing by international banks, the choice of export products with lower variance in price would appear attractive even on the market criterion for the selection of goods for export. Did the emphasis on the export of agricultural products make sense in this context, even assuming that the choice should be dictated, wherever possible, by market signals?

Consider the following theoretical decision model. A country has two choices, export A or export B. The prices P_A and P_B have different degrees of volatility. Suppose there are two likely sets

Table 3.7   Potential profit per unit of export (= price − cost)

	Event I (Probability 0.80)	Event II (Probability 0.20)
Export *A*	10	−1
Export *B*	3	2

of prices: $\{P_A = 11,\ P_B = 4\}$ with probability p_1 and $\{P_A = 0,\ P_B = 3\}$ with probability p_2. These probabilities are known to be 0.80 and 0.20, respectively. Production cost is 1 for both the products *A* and *B*. Then the decisionmaker has the matrix of potential gains shown in Table 3.7.

The expected values of profits from exports of products *A* and *B* are as follows:

$$E\{A\} = 0.80 \times 10 + 0.20 \times (-1) = 7.80$$

$$E\{B\} = 0.80 \times 3 - 0.20 \times 2 = 2.80$$

The average rate of return from investing in export good *A* is much higher than the corresponding rate for betting on *B*. If bank lending were available, a country could borrow to tide it over in case Event II occurred. On average, it would earn enough to be able to service that loan, and still have some left over from the average profit of 7.80 to enjoy a higher level of material well being than the country would obtain from the choice of *B*. However, if the probabilities of Events I and II are not known to banks, and they have no facility of calculating the level of risk, borrowing for survival in the unlikely event (probability = 0.20) of a collapse in the international price of *A* might not be an available option. Hence the choice of *B* would be prudent. This choice would maximise the minimum gain, hence it is called a maximin strategy, should the more pessimistic prognosis for prices obtain (Baumol, 1977, pp. 460–1). By this maximin criterion, economists with no ideological aversion to markets might still recommend B, the commodity which would guarantee a more stable earning. Is the Chilean policy of developing export agriculture in preference to concentrating efforts on other commodities, especially mining and metals, consistent with risk-aversion as outlined above?

Table 3.8 Indices of price movements, constant dollars, 1977–9 = 100

Year	COMM33	Agriculture	Metals and minerals
1950	144	154	131
1951	146	152	138
1952	132	128	156
1953	127	125	148
1954	138	139	144
1955	135	129	165
1956	135	128	170
1957	126	123	146
1958	108	105	128
1959	113	109	131
1960	111	106	130
1961	105	99	128
1962	105	99	126
1963	113	111	122
1964	117	109	148
1965	113	97	166
1966	114	95	174
1967	106	95	144
1968	114	101	158
1969	122	107	171
1970	115	102	162
1971	100	91	128
1972	97	92	116
1973	123	118	141
1974	141	138	155
1975	100	96	117
1976	105	104	112
1977	114	119	105
1978	92	93	91
1979	97	92	104
1980	102	98	106
1981	90	85	99
1982	80	74	93

Source: Labys and Pollak (1984) Table 1.4.

First consider Table 3.8, showing price movements of developing country exports, expressed as index of purchasing power of these exports. The aggregate of 33 commodities below, COMM33, excludes energy. The Metals and Minerals index excludes petroleum, which experienced a sudden rise in fortune in the early 1970s.

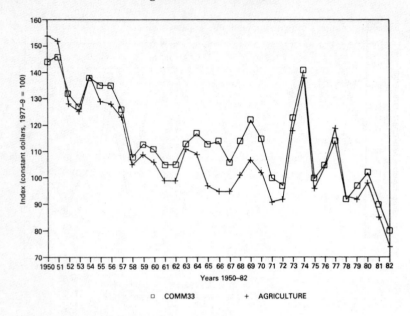

Figure 3.1 Price movements, agriculture and COMM33

It appears at first sight that the prices of agricultural products exhibit greater variation than COMM33 and no less instability than Metals and Minerals. Computing yearly percentage price changes for 1951 to 1982 from the data in Table 3.8, we note that these changes were greater in Agriculture than in COMM33 for 19 out of 32 years. However, the percentage value of yearly price changes in Agriculture exceeded that observed in Metals and Minerals in only half of the years (in 16 out of 32). Looking at the magnitude of price fluctuations, agriculture does not appear to have been more volatile than either of the above commodity groups (See Figures 3.1 and 3.2). Within the logic of market economics, if agriculture is treated as a special case requiring discouragement of land use in export agriculture and cash crops, even for a country enjoying comparative advantage in these crops, then it has to be demonstrated that agricultural prices fluctuate more wildly than the price of other export commodities. That does not appear to be the case. It appears on the other hand that the price movements in Metals and Agriculture have

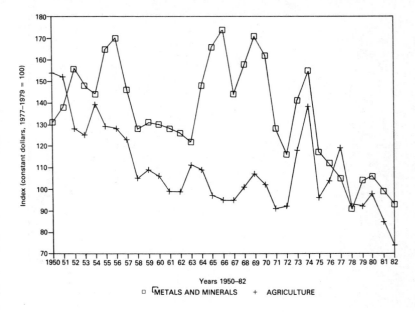

Figure 3.2   Price movements, agriculture and metals and minerals

moved in opposite directions in almost half of the years (see Figure 3.2). The aggregate export earnings from Agriculture and Metals together would be less volatile if the share of the two industries converged. This indeed was the trend in the 1980s (see Table 3.4). The combined price index of Agriculture and Metals is shown in Figure 3.3, using two sets of weights, corresponding to the ratio of Agriculture to Metal export in the early 1970s and in the late 1980s. The variance is lower in the second period.

3.4   CHILEAN FORESTRY

An outline

Turning back to Table 3.5, we note that the contribution of forestry products to Chilean exports remained small throughout the 1980s, accounting for less than 0.3 per cent of agricultural

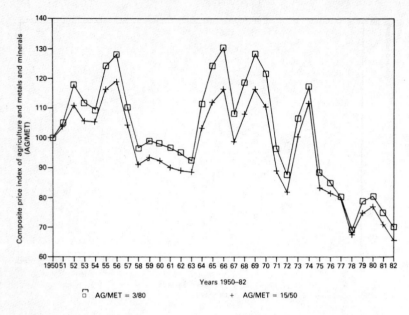

Years 1950–82

◻ AG/MET = 3/80   + AG/MET = 15/50

Figure 3.3   Ratio of agriculture to metals and minerals: 3/80 and 15/50, price index set at 100 in 1950

exports. Starting from a low base of 2.1 million dollars in 1981, forestry's direct contribution to exports reached only 2.6 million by 1988. Earnings from forestry exports have fluctuated for almost two decades, but always remained low. What is remarkable about these figures is the relative ease with which production for export can be increased in response to short-term policy objectives, often determined by market signals. Another aspect of the statistics about forestry exports is the increasing contribution of wood products, pulp and cellulose fibre in recent years. The figures for direct forestry exports do not give a true indication of the export contribution of the forestry sector. The aggregate exports of forestry, wood products (*maderas*), and celulose, etc. (*papel, celulosa y derivados del papel*) had risen from around 40.2 million dollars in 1971 to 730.3 million dollars by 1988 (Banco Central de Chile, *Boletín Mensual*).

Dependence on markets has grown with time. Virtually the entire growth in forestry in recent years has taken place in the private sector. Between 1980 and 1985, the forest area planted by the national Forestry Corporation declined from 85 000 to

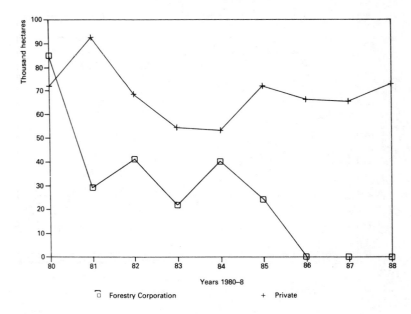

Figure 3.4 Forestry area planted yearly

24 000 hectares. The Corporation planted nothing in any of the following three years. The yearly area planted by individuals and private enterprises remained positive, bounded between a high of 94 000 and a low of 72 000 hectares (see Figure 3.4).

The rate at which trees are cut down affects not only the owners of the forests, but also other members of society through the consequential effects on the environment. The question that occurs is this: do rates of depletion of forests and programmes of afforestation, which are primarily driven by market signals, adequately reflect the interests of present society and those of future generations?

Private investment

In selecting one project from amongst a list of projects, a profit-maximising private investor would favour the one yielding the highest rate of return on investment. Assuming that there are no tax distortions in calculations of the rate of return, the private choice would favour the most efficient use of investment capital.

Table 3.9   Cash flow of investment

Period	Investment cost		Revenue		Running cost		Social cost		Cash flow Private		Social	
	A	B	A	B	A	B	A	B	A	B	A	B
0	1.0	1.0	0.0	0.0	0.0	0.0	0.0	0.0	−1.0	−1.0	−1.0	−1.0
1	0.0	0.0	0.8	0.8	0.1	0.1	0.0	0.0	0.7	0.7	0.7	0.7
2	0.0	0.0	0.5	0.5	0.1	0.1	0.0	0.0	0.4	0.4	0.4	0.4
3	0.0	0.0	0.3	0.3	0.1	0.1	0.1	0.0	0.2	0.2	0.1	0.2

Society as a whole would thus gain in terms of efficiency. This logic is dented when there is a divergence between private and social costs. This divergence could arise if the implementation of the project in question affected members of society other than those concerned with the related production and consumption. If trees are cut down now, the resulting effects of atmospheric changes and soil erosion could visit all members of society. Even future generations might have to pay for this activity, in which they could not have a say.

Suppose the social costs of forestry are incurred over time. Thus the rates of discount of future gains from forestry are different between private investors and society. The market rate of return is not the same as the social rate of return, as illustrated by the simple example in Table 3.9. It is assumed that there is 1 dollar available for investment, and the choice is between project A and B. Project A has environmental effects which can be quantified in money terms, but Project B has no such effects. Return accrues over a period of time (see Table 3.9).

The net present value (NPV) of a project is obtained by summing the private cash flow over the period of duration of the project, discounted at a rate r. The marginal productivity of capital from the investor's point of view is that rate of interest, called the internal rate of return (IRR) at which NPV is equal to 0. We note that the private rate of return is 18.17 per cent for both the above projects, but the social rate of return is lower at 13.16 per cent for Project A. This project entails a social cost, and hence the rate of return is lower for society.

The above analysis would suggest that there are two ways of approaching investment decisions concerning activities which have social externalities. If there is a social cost of the activity, private investors could be taxed at a rate such that the net private rate of return equals the social rate of return. The second alternative is to keep in the social sector those investment projects which manifest substantial externalities. The recent trend in Chile has been to turn forestry over to private enterprise; there has been no corresponding effort at taxing investment in this sector to reflect its social externalities.

Even if there were such an effort, it would have failed to achieve the purpose of securing the interests of future generations who are likely to be affected by current activities in forestry. Articulation of their interest entails an explicit commitment to confronting the question of distributive justice, an issue which was never the central concern of the Pinochet regime. The reason for this requirement lies in the nature of discounting the future which forms the basis of the environmental tax calculations outlined above.

Time discount

The above exercise in computing the rate of return assumed that benefits and losses now matter more than they would do if they occurred in the future. Thus a dollar at hand now is more valuable than a dollar at hand later. Hence a positive rate of discount is assumed for the future. For an individual, it might make sense to assume this on the ground of diminishing marginal utility of income coupled with productivity of savings allowing for growth in future consumption (Olson and Bailey, 1981). If the consumer were indifferent between consumption now and consumption in the future, this would lead to postponement of consumption until the last moment prior to death, thus allowing for the greatest amount of accumulation. This kind of behaviour is not observed. There is an empirical case for assuming a positive rate of discount for an individual maximising his lifetime consumption stream. There is no normative judgement involved.

When a discount is placed on the consumption of future generations, that is an expression of a normative view. Also, calculations based on discounting time far into the future, well beyond any individual's own expected lifetime, can produce absurd results (Pearce, 1975). An illustration of the inappropriateness of extending the logic of the calculation of the rate of return for private investment into investment decisions involving the long-term future of society is given below (Price, 1989, p. 110):

> Consider an exploitation project which yields net revenue of Rs 1 million at the end of every year from the first to the tenth. After that time, the forest cover has been removed entirely, in consequence of which catastrophic flooding and erosion cause losses estimated at Rs 1000 million. The IRR [internal rate of return] of this outrageous project (there is only one) is +99.4%.
>
> The explanation is simple and dreadful: the large future costs must be reduced to the same magnitude as the early modest revenues. This can only be done by discounting very rapidly. In fact, if the scale of damage had been greater, the IRR would have been higher, and the investment would have appeared even more desirable!

Investment decisions which involve no one but the decision-maker himself are amenable to economic analyses deriving from the logic of the market place. Discounting the future requires an explanation if generations other than the decisionmaker's own are concerned.

Fairness between generations

There are two ways of viewing this problem of inter-generational externality: (1) Democracy entails taking into account only the views of those who vote. Therefore, present decisions need be based only on the preferences of those now living and able to take a position on issues. (2) Fairness entails that privileges and responsibilities must not derive arbitrarily. Thus the access to environmental amenities or natural resources based on some such criterion as the date of birth is unfair.

The first view gives a particular definition of democracy. It provides no argument for the legitimacy of that concept of demo-cratic decision. There is an extreme Benthamite view of society that lurks behind a notion that aggregation of the interests of those who live in society is the best we can do about articulating a view of the communal interest. Consider Bentham (quoted by Arblaster, 1987, p. 65):

The community is a fictitious *body*, composed of the individual persons who are considered as constituting as it were its *members*. The interest of the community then is, what? – the sum of the interests of the several members who compose it.

The Benthamite quest for unanimity as the only way to formulate social choice has led 'liberal' economists down the path to paralysis in evaluating policies entailing a community view. Large strides in the provision of public goods – sewerage and water, health care and schooling – have been made in capitalist societies only because the Benthamite formula has been ignored from time to time. This formula fails again in providing a framework for discussing the question of inter-generational distribution. A problem is that individual rankings of policy, when it comes to inter-generational distribution of rights and privileges, do not appear to satisfy the concept of rationality characterising liberal economic thought. The following example might help (Ng, 1989, p. 237):

> Suppose that a chemical has been invented which if released into the air will clean up the atmosphere and make us healthy, able to enjoy life better and not get any older. But it will also make us all sterile (but sexually still active, if not more so) and die painlessly after one hundred years. Suppose also that everyone regards the better health, etc. as more than compensating for the inability to have any more children. So all existing persons will be better off and no new person will be born. Should the chemical be released? The answer is yes if we ignore prospective persons.

Consider the above case. Even if, as individuals, we regard 'the better health, etc. as more than compensating for the inability to have any more children', we might not regard the cessation of the human race through the release of Ng's chemical as an acceptable outcome. There is a seeming contradiction in our choice amongst alternatives. This contradiction arises in an attempt to put individuals' choice of social options in the same category as their choice of options available to them as individuals. People may well regard the two sets of problems in a different light, and thus violate rationality of choice as postulated in liberal economics.

The idea of a social contract, where it is in the interest of individuals to consent to social action, has appealed to economists as a way out of the conundrum posed by the need for public action to provide social goods not supplied by the market. The operative clause is the individual interest (see Rousseau, 1974 reprint, p. 49):

> The engagements which bind us to the social body are obligatory only because they are mutual; and their nature is such that in fulfilling them we cannot work for others without also working for ourselves.

'The engagements', the social contract, which 'bind us to the social body' are arrived at voluntarily. It is through a novel concept of the definition of the word 'voluntary' that John Rawls arrived at a theory of distributive justice, capturing the imagination of social democrats.

Rawls (1971) postulates a hypothetical construct, the veil of ignorance, defining 'The Original Position' (pp. 118–92) in which the social contract is drawn up. It is characterised by a state of affairs in which the contracting parties are ignorant of those particular facts which might induce them to advance personal interest as social interest. For example (p. 137):

> First of all, no one knows his place in society, his class position, or social status; nor does he know his fortune in the distribution of natural assets and abilities, his intelligence and strength, and the like. Nor, again, does anyone know his conception of the good, the particulars of his rational plan of life, or even the special features of his psychology such as his aversion to risk or liability to optimism and pessimism. More than this, I assume that the parties do not know the particular circumstances of their own society. That is, they do not know its economic situation, or the level of civilization and culture it has been able to achieve. The persons in the original position have no information as to which generation they belong.

Starting with the above artificial construct, Rawls goes on to derive a set of rules for distributive justice that citizens in the above condition of ignorance would voluntarily agree upon.

Since the parties to the contract do not even know – namely, set aside from their mind any knowledge of – the generation to which they belong, the contract provides a basis for discussing the inter-generational allocation problem (Grout, 1977).

Despite the enthusiasm which the Rawlsian theory has generated, it fails a crucial test of fairness, that the antecedent calculations of self-interest be based on relevant information needed to make those calculations. Consider the following argument (Dworkin, 1978, p. 19):

> Suppose I did not know the value of my painting on Monday; if you had offered me $100 for it then I would have accepted. On Tuesday I discovered it was valuable. You cannot argue that it would be fair for the courts to make me sell it to you for $100 on Wednesday. It may be my good fortune that you did not ask me on Monday, but that does not justify coercion against me later.

Dworkin does not do so, but he might have put his case even more strongly: 'Even if you had no knowledge on Monday that my painting was valuable and would fetch substantially more than the amount ($100) for which I agreed to sell you that object in ignorance of its market value, "it would not be fair for the courts to make me sell it to you for $100 on Wednesday".' The reason for holding this view can be found in the last sentence of the quotation above. It is simply good fortune for you that I had agreed to sell the painting to you for $100 on Monday, before the market price came to my attention on Tuesday. The allocation of goods, according to our contract, was determined by the intervention of a random factor. If fairness is assumed to entail a non-arbitrary allocation of rights and privileges, the Rawlsian prescription loses its shine (Swanton, 1981).

A plea for natural resource exploitation and environmental protection, appealing to an intuitive argument which dismisses the concept of solipsism inherent in the approaches cited above, has been made by Brian Barry (quoted in Streeten, 1986, p. 13):

> if I try to analyse the source of my own strong conviction that we should be wrong to take risks with the continuation of human life, I find that it does not lie in any sense of injury to the interests of people who will not get born but rather a sense

of its cosmic impertinence – that we should be grossly abusing our position by taking it upon ourselves to put a term on human life and possibilities.

It is difficult to find any logic in the above view within the confines of the intellectual capital of liberal economics. Hence the Chilean government has seen it fit to hand over an ever greater portion of the activity of exploiting forestry resources, with all its long-term environmental consequences, to the private sector. Even if it is accepted that neither natural resources nor environmental amenities would need to be bequeathed to future generations in the exact state as they exist now, a social consensus must be found about the rules which should circumscribe market behaviour in economic spheres holding consequences for those not yet born. A minimum requirement would be to make sure that the opportunities were equally distributed between generations. It is not unreasonable to argue that society should intervene in the markets to make sure that 'we should leave future generations the same productive capacity and therefore the same opportunities that we now enjoy. If we deplete some exhaustible resource, we would have to compensate for this by some technological innovation or capital accumulation that makes any given amount [of that resource yield more output], or substitutes some other source for the depleted resource' (Streeten, 1986, p. 11). The same argument could also be advanced for the environment. If we damage it now, we must do so only at a pace which can be reversed. If part of the cost of that reversal is to be charged to the future, the reason must be articulated. Perhaps it might be maintained that, if future generations are richer, they should pay towards the cost for cleaning up the environment even for that damage which is attributable to us. Also it might be argued that citizens of poorer countries gain greater marginal utility from consumption now than their counterparts in richer societies; hence, the discount rate will be greater in poorer countries. These are matters which require open discussion in society, because the act of leaving things to the market is an abdication of responsibility.

3.5 CONCLUSIONS

The Chilean economy has come to rely more on price signals of the international market place. A consequence for agriculture and forestry is that these activities have been opened up for trade with the world. In the process, contrary to the expectations of those who are pessimistic about market-led growth policies, the country has not become more dependent on food imports. It has become more reliant on food exports for earning foreign exchange, but this trend has not made export earnings more volatile, again defying the predictions of market pessimism. In the early 1970s, almost 80 per cent of the value of exports was attributable to copper. Agriculture accounted for a mere 3 per cent of the total exports. By the end of the 1980s, dependence on copper was reduced to about 50 per cent, while agriculture's share of the total rose between 4 and 5 times during that period. This convergence of the export shares has reduced the volatility of the export prices faced by Chile: greater reliance on market prices to determine the commodities for export has, paradoxically, made Chile less vulnerable to price fluctuations in the international markets. The difficulty with market-led policies lies in the government's dedication to an economic theory which is too impoverished to answer questions of distributive justice. We have considered one aspect of that shortcoming here. One of the issues that needs to be confronted is the calculation of compensation to future generations through technological innovation or whatever for the use of environmental and other resources. The trend towards privatisation in forestry raises questions of intergenerational fairness for which no answer can be found in the economic doctrine which informs Chilean policy.

Note

1. I am indebted to David Hojman and Liu Aying for comments.

References:

Ackerlof, G. A. (1970) 'The Market for "Lemons": Quality Uncertainty and the Market Mechanism', *Quarterly Journal of Economics* (August 1970) 488–500.

Anderson, D. and Fishwick, R. (1984) *Fuelwood Consumption and Deforestation in African Countries*, World Bank Staff Paper, no. 704, (Washington, D.C.: World Bank).

Arblaster, A. (1987) *Democracy* (Milton Keynes: Open University Press).

Banco Central de Chile, *Boletín Mensual*, various numbers.

Baumol, W. J. (1977) *Economic Theory and Operations Analysis* (New Jersey: Prentice-Hall) 4th edn. pp. 460–1.

Dworkin, R. (1978) 'The Original Position', in Norman Daniels (ed.), *Reading Rawls* (Oxford: Blackwell) pp. 16–53.

Grout, P. (1977) 'A Rawlsian Intertemporal Consumption Rule', *Review of Economic Studies*, vol. 44, pp. 337–46.

Helleiner, G. K. (1986) 'Outward Orientation, Import Instability and African Economic Growth: An Empirical Investigation', in S. Lal and F. Stewart (eds), *Theory and Reality in Development* (London: Macmillan).

Hojman, D. (ed.) (1990) *Neo-liberal Agriculture in Rural Chile* (London: Macmillan).

Hojman, D. (1992) *Chile: The Political Economy of Development and Democracy in the 1990s* (London: Macmillan).

Labys, W. C. and Pollak, P. K. (1984) *Commodity Models for Forecasting and Policy Analysis* (London: Croom Helm).

Little, I. M. D. (1982) *Economic Development* (New York: Basic Books).

Ng, Y. K. (1989) 'What Should We Do About Future Generations?', *Economics and Philosophy*, vol. 5, pp. 235–53.

Olson, M. and Bailey, M. J. (1981) 'Positive Time Preference', *Journal of Political Economy*, vol. 89, no. 1, pp. 1–25.

Pearce, D., Markandya, A. and Barbier, E. B. (1989) *Blueprint for a Green Economy* (London: Earthscan).

Pearce, I. (1975) 'Resource Conservation and the Market Mechanism', in D. W. Pearce and J. Rose (eds), *The Economics of Natural Resource Depletion* (London: Macmillan, 1975) pp. 191–203.

Price, C. (1989) *The Theory and Practice of Forest Economics* (Oxford: Blackwell).

Rawls, J. (1971) *A Theory of Justice* (Cambridge, Mass.: Harvard University Press).

Rousseau, J.-J. (1974) *The Social Contract or Principles of Political Right* (revised reprint and translation by C. M. Sherover) (New York: Meridian Books).

Sarris, A. H. (1988) 'Food Security and International Security', paper presented at the Workshop on Economic Aspects of International Security (London: Centre for Economic Policy Research) (March).

Streeten, P. (1986) 'What Do We Owe the Future?', *Resources Policy*, vol. 12, no. 1 (March) pp. 4–16.

Swanton, C. (1981) 'Is Difference Principle a Principle of Justice?', *Mind*, vol. 90, pp. 415–21.

Tversky, A. and Kahneman, D. (1981) 'The Framing of Decisions and the Psychology of Choice', *Science*, vol. 211, pp. 453–8; reprinted in Jon Elster (ed.), *Rational Choice* (Oxford: Blackwell, 1986).
Winters, L. A. (1988) 'The So-Called "Non-Economic" Objectives of Agricultural Policy', Working Paper 52 (Paris: OECD) (April).

4 Landowners and the State: Beyond Agrarian Reform and Counter-reform

Patricio Silva

4.1 INTRODUCTION

This chapter focuses on the relationship between landowner organisations and the state during the military government, stressing the main political and economic factors which determinated its evolution. In addition, it indicates some of the new features this relationship is beginning to acquire, following the restoration of democratic rule in March 1990.

The nature of landowners–state relations in Chile since 1973, however, becomes difficult to understand unless its evolution during the decades preceding the military takeover is also considered. The land reform, in particular, constituted for most landowners a highly traumatic experience. This experience was not only important in determining their attitude towards the military government, but also in keeping alive for a long time their resistance to the eventual restoration of democracy.

4.2 LANDOWNERS AND THE STATE: AN ERA OF CONFRONTATION

Since the late 1940s relations between landowner organisations and the state had been characterised by continuous clashes, produced by the landowners' discontent about agrarian policies, and by their unwillingness to improve the living conditions of the peasantry.

During the 1940s and 1950s landowner organisations repeatedly accused the state of adopting strong pro-industrialist positions, to the detriment of development in the agrarian sector. In their view, the state was applying an 'anti-policy' towards agriculture by fixing low prices for their products and by not protecting it sufficiently from subsidised foreign competition (Carrière, 1980; Wright, 1982; Zeitlin and Ratcliff, 1986).

In the period 1964 to 1973, land reform became the central focus of conflict between landowners and the state (Gómez, 1972). The expropriation of land by the state, and its active support of the unionisation of peasants, took place *vis-à-vis* an increasing social and political polarisation in the countryside.

The state accused the agrarian entrepreneurs of being one of the main obstacles to the country's modernisation. Leaning upon the structuralist thesis, the governments of Eduardo Frei and Salvador Allende presented the application of land reform and the elimination of the *latifundia* system as a prerequisite for the solution of the development problems facing society (CIDA, 1965; Lehmann, 1974). During the land reform, a negative and stereotyped image of the agrarian entrepreneurs was officially spread. The landowners as a whole were presented as not different from the traditional *latifundistas*, owning land simply for social prestige, and not in order to produce the food needed by the population. This, despite the fact that during that period a significant sector of middle and large landowners existed which had adopted modern productive methods and contributed an important share of total food production (Barraclough and Fernández, 1974).

In addition, the agrarian question was often explained in simplistic terms, to the point that everything that was wrong became identified by some with the landowners themselves. In their view, *the* solution to all the problems affecting agriculture involved the elimination of the agrarian entrepreneurs.

Under the *Unidad Popular* government, the objective of eliminating the *latifundia* acquired an important political dimension. The parties of the government coalition regarded the existence of a landed oligarchy as a serious obstacle to the instauration of socialism. The agrarian entrepreneurs, fighting for their very right to exist, offered an extremely tough opposition to the Allende government, being also some of the most active supporters of military intervention in September 1973 (Kay, 1978).

4.3 LANDOWNERS AND THE MILITARY: FROM EUPHORIA TO SCEPTICISM

The overthrow of Allende produced a general sense of joy among entrepreneurial circles. Even the official announcement of the application of a tough economic policy, severe credit restrictions, and the elimination of state support for the productive sectors, initially constituted no a major deterrant to continued support for the new authorities (Campero, 1984).

After the coup, an increasing depoliticisation in the relationship between agrarian entrepreneurs and the state took place. The politico–ideological battle which had accompanied the land reform was over. The military government showed from the very beginning its readiness to grant some of the landowners' demands.

The landowners constituted one of the entrepreneurial groups most disposed to accepting the sacrifices demanded by the realignment of productive sectors to the new economic guidelines. The recovery of their land, and the dismantling of the peasant movement led them to express their trust and optimism in all the measures adopted by the government. In spite of the risks associated to the new economic policy (reduction of tariffs, elimination of state protection, etc.) the agrarian entrepreneurs initially accepted without any objections the new economic model. The president of the *Sociedad Nacional de Agricultura* (SNA), Alfonso Márquez de la Plata, said at the opening of the Santiago International Exhibition (FISA):

> A new era has began for Chilean agriculture. Our country will have to compete with other nations, most of which possess more adequate natural and economic resources. Nevertheless, Chilean agriculture does accept the challenge (*El campesino*, November 1973, p. 17).

The landowners also expressed their support by renouncing their right to receive a state indemnity for the expropriation of their properties during the land reform. They presented this decision as their contribution to the so-called 'national reconstruction' proposed by the new authorities. However, by the end of 1974 the official discourse on 'national reconstruction' had almost disappeared, while some entrepreneurial sectors became disconcerted and confused as the real consequences of the economic policy became apparent.

Moreover, the unconditional withdrawal by the entrepreneurial class from the political and economic management of the country led to the formation of a new structure of decisionmaking centred around a civilian neo-liberal technocracy (the so-called 'Chicago Boys'). This team of young economists was not only planning to introduce radical changes in the functioning of the economy, but also a comprehensive transformation of the entire society.

The application in 1975 by the neo-liberal technocracy of an orthodox stabilisation policy (the so-called 'shock treatment') produced a severe economic crisis. This created a cleavage in the entrepreneurial consensus which had previously emerged around the slogan of national reconstruction. The policies applied by the neo-liberal technocracy could not any longer rely on the general support of entrepreneurs' organisations. For instance, industrialists openly expressed their preference for an economic strategy based on more gradual change (Campero, 1984).

For a while, the military government was able to calm the emerging dissidence amongst entrepreneurial circles by stressing the temporary nature of the economic difficulties generated by the stabilisation policy. Stabilisation was presented as painful, but necessary, after which the entrepreneurs should be able to achieve their productive goals.

4.4 AGRARIAN ENTREPRENEURS AND THE 'CHICAGO BOYS'

At the beginning, concern among landowners was expressed only within their own organisations.

After 1976, however, many landowner organisations started to make public their doubts about the economic path being followed by the neo-liberal technocracy. A growing mobilisation among agrarian entrepreneurs who had been negatively affected by foreign competition and the lack of state support took place. This mobilisation showed two particular features.

First, it was not endorsed by all the landowner organisations. The economic policy had produced a serious breach in the traditional unity among organisations, because of its differentiated impact on agrarian producers. Although the majority had experienced a marked deterioration in their economic situation, there were also many agrarian producers who successfully adapted themselves to the new rules of the game, becoming strong supporters of the neo-liberal policies.

Secondly, the protests against the economic policy did not acquire a clear political connotation. Despite their criticism of the economic model, the landowner organisations constantly expressed their loyalty, political support and gratitude towards the military government.

The agrarian entrepreneurs demanded the adoption of what they called 'corrective measures', such as a reduction of the interest rate, which was identified as a serious obstacle to increased investment in agriculture. They also argued that due to severe losses of capital during the agrarian reform, the sector now needed special treatment with regard to the granting of loans.

The agrarian entrepreneurs also demanded that the military government not go along with its plan to allow imports of agricultural products at *dumping* prices. They stated that they were not opposed to competing with foreign producers, but that this competition had to take place under fair conditions. In their view it was the task of the government to avoid 'unfair' foreign competition – i.e. imports of products which had been strongly subsidised by their own governments.

The agrarian producers specially criticised the massive imports of wheat which had seriously depressed cereal prices in the internal market. They also argued that increasing dependence on imports of foreign wheat constituted a major threat to the food security of the population and, hence, to the country's national security. With this, the landowners attempted to link their own demands with a very sensitive theme in military circles. They asked the government to consider wheat as a strategic product and actively to support its production in Chile. The aim for the country was to become self-sufficient.

The landowners' complaints, however, were ignored by the economic authorities. The neo-liberal economic team presented the 'technocratisation of decision-making' as a guarantee of the adoption of rational economic policies. They argued that the sneaky defence of particular interests was to the detriment of the general interest of the nation (O'Brien, 1981; Vergara, 1985). As

Minister Pablo Baraona put it: 'We have never consulted the agrarian producers for the adoption of any measure. Our decisions are not negotiated, and the government will not allow any pressure during the implementation of its policies' (*La Tercera*, 29 July 1977).

The neo-liberal technocracy also mobilised the official press to refute the landowners' demands. In *El Mercurio*, for example, they were accused of pining for old socialist practices, such as state protection and the easy availability of subsidised credits. 'Eventual compliance by the government with the private entrepreneurs' demands – of a clear statist nature – could bring the country back to socialism' (*El Mercurio*, 12 December 1976).

It is obvious that the Chicago Boys' inflexibility was made possible only by the authoritarian nature of the regime, which did not depend on the achievement of a broad consensus in the population to govern.

A good example of neo-liberal arrogance and political insensitivity in dealing with entrepreneurial sectors, is the so-called 'milk conflict' of 1977, between some organisations of agrarian producers and government policymakers. This conflict was originated by the government's decision to introduce a large reduction in tariffs on milk imports which were adversely affecting domestic interests. Landowner organisations such as the *Confederación de Productores Agrícolas* (CPA) protested, arguing that foreign milk was strongly subsidised by the European Community, and hence that this did not constitute fair competition. Moreover, imports of milk would threaten the survival of the national milk industry. In a meeting at the Ministry of Economic Affairs, the leaders of agrarian entrepreneurs were ridiculed by a high ranking official, who told them that there was no solution but 'to eat up the cows' (Gómez, 1982: 121–6).

The landowner organisations tried desperately to make a distinction between the civilian neo-liberal technocracy and the military rulers. So each time they protested against some aspect of the economic policy, they explicitly directed their criticism against the Chicago Boys, but simultaneously expressed their commitment towards the 'government of the armed forces'. This, however, availed them nothing. The alliance between the military and the neo-liberal technocrats had became very close, and the former showed at that point no disposition whatsoever to interfere in the formulation and implementation of economic policy.

4.5　NEO-LIBERALISM AND PRODUCTIVE DIFFERENTIATION

It is well known that the application of the neo-liberal model generated a process of differentiation within the agricultural sector. This process of economic differentiation did affect the solid unity among landowner organisations which had been cast during their battle against land reform.

As Campero (1984) has pointed out, tension between different landowner organisations was also the result of different evaluations about the degree of consolidation of the new economic scheme. According to SNA, the introduction of neo-liberal guidelines in agriculture was a *fait accompli*, so any discussion about a possible reformulation of it following entrepreneurs' demands was pointless. In other words, SNA accepted the strategy based on specialisation of agriculture and its reorientation toward external markets. CPA, on the contrary, persisted in its defence of the principle of 'integral development', by which economic growth of agriculture had to be reached through modernisation and increases of production in all the main components of Chilean agriculture.

SNA openly criticised the combative attitude adopted by CPA, arguing that this would severely damage unity among agrarian entrepreneurs. This criticism reflected also different ways of acting by these organisations. CPA cherished its close contact with its members and its great capability for mobilisation of its bases. SNA, on the contrary, traditionally (with the exception of the land reform period) conducted negotiations with governments 'from above', always trying to avoid controversial publicity or the radicalisation of conflict by mobilising its members.

4.6　FROM CRISIS TO AGRICULTURAL RECOVERY

The economic crisis in 1981–2 however, did produce an increasing rapprochement among organisations of landowners. Initially, SNA supported the official thesis that the crisis was only temporary. But the rapid and sustained deterioration of the economic situation forced it to reconsider its position and to recognise the structural nature of the recession. In late 1981 SNA also began to demand the reformulation of agrarian policy, when influential enterprises such as the sugar producer CRAV and several fruit export companies went bankrupt.

In order to mobilise public opinion in their favour, landowners in 1981 hired the agricultural expert Clifford M. Hardin, former US Secretary of Agriculture, to elaborate an independent diagnosis of the problems facing Chilean agriculture and possible solutions. In his final report, delivered at the beginning of 1982, he recommended a major increase in flexibility and a relaxation in the application of neo-liberal policies and the adoption of fiscal and financial measures in support of agrarian producers. By that time, most landowners were no longer able to meet their financial commitments with banks. The debt of agrarian producers with private financial institutions and the state amounted to 2600 million dollars (*El campesino*, March 1982).

The government could no longer ignore the fact that agriculture was in crisis. Agricultural GDP experienced drops of 2.1 per cent in 1982 and 3.6 per cent in 1983. The total cultivated area decreased to 860 000 hectares, from a historical average of 1 200 000 hectares (*Revista del Campo*, 12 March 1990).

But agriculture was not the only sector negatively affected by the crisis. The rest of the economy also suffered. Pinochet finally discharged the neo-liberal economic team and adopted a more pragmatic policy.

From 1983 onwards, the government took a series of measures to confront the crisis in agriculture. Additional commercial and fiscal facilities were granted to stimulate exports. A new line of credit was opened to agrarian entrepreneurs to modernise their productive units. Tough anti-dumping measures were adopted, and many agricultural products (such a wheat and milk) were protected by import tariffs. Even more important and urgent for agrarian entrepreneurs, their debts with banks were renegotiated (Echeñique, 1990, pp. 148–9).

After 1983, the economy in general, and particularly agriculture, experienced a strong recovery as a result of the new policies and an improved situation in international markets. The reactivation of agriculture led to the demobilisation of landowner organisations after their successful opposition to neo-liberal policies; they were clearly satisfied with the new economic measures. Improvement of the economic situation also healed most of the wounds inflicted by internal disputes during the pre-crisis period.

However, during the crisis a large political opposition against the military government had become well established. This produced a renewed and united political support from the agrarian entrepreneurs for Pinochet, afraid of the consequences of possible changes in the political and economic spheres. During the 1988 referendum and the 1989 presidential elections, landowner organisations played an active role in the official campaigns, expressing gratitude towards Pinochet and confidence in the economic perspectives for agriculture.

4.7 DEMOCRATISATION AND THE SEARCH FOR CONSENSUS

Since the restoration of democratic rule in March 1990, the Aylwin administration has been trying to reach a broad consensus among the country's main social and political forces on key issues, such as taxation, labour legislation, and on diverse economic matters. The *Concertación* (government coalition) is well aware of the fact that a situation of naked confrontation could easily jeopardise its efforts to consolidate the democratic system.

The new authorities seem also to be aware of the urgent need to eliminate the fears and distrust of agrarian entrepreneurs towards the political forces now in power. The *Concertación* is constituted around Christian Democrats and Socialists, the two main political forces responsible for the application of land reform in 1964–73.

As Gómez and Echeñique have pointed out:

> to solve the existing problems in Chilean agriculture and obtain the support of agrarian entrepreneurs for the goal of increasing production and exports, a broad political pact is needed in which all parties will have to make concessions. Failing to resolve apparent contradictions by democratic negotiation would lead either to a process of violent transformation or to an equally violent return to authoritarianism (1988, p. 274).

Actually, it seems unlikely that the old confrontation between state and agrarian entrepreneurs of the land reform years will be re-fought. During the presidential campaign, the *Concertación* made clear that a new version of the land reform was not on the agenda. Its own assessment of the experience was not completely favourable. It is categorically stated that the democratic state would not discriminate against any economic activity and that the right of private property, in all its forms, should be fully guaranteed. On agricultural development, a policy was promised which constituted a continuation of that applied during the last years of the military government. It was formulated in cautious technocratic terms, avoiding the mention of any aspect related to social and political dimensions or to the land reform (*Concertación*, 1989, pp. 20–1).

The new government has also shown great caution in the appointment of high-ranking officials at the Ministry of Agriculture. None of them played a prominent role during land reform in 1964–73; none could be described as 'controversial'. Moreover, they are mainly recruited from the most moderate sectors of the government coalition. Some of them are independent. Almost all of them are not *políticos*, but highly specialised technocrats, experts in the specific fields in which they are in charge. Key institutions such as INIA, INDAP, CONAF, and SAG, are headed by two agronomists, a forestry expert and a veterinary doctor, respectively (*El Mercurio*, 12 March 1990). The nomination of Juan Agustín Figueroa as Minister of Agriculture above all appears to reflect the government's intention to maintain a fluid channel of communication with agrarian entrepreneurs. Figueroa is a lawyer, a member of the moderate Radical Party, who was not even known among circles of social scientists dealing with the agrarian reform and its aftermath. The reason for this unexpected nomination seems to be that he is a landowner who has political and social skills, and the right connections needed to conduct in a non-antagonistic way the state relations with landowner organisations.

Peasant unionisation does not today constitute a major source of conflict between state and landowner organisations, as was the case before September 1973. During the military government, because of state repression, high rates of unemployment, and new labour legislation, the bargaining capacity of peasant organisations was almost totally destroyed. This persuaded many agrarian entrepreneurs to invest in their lands and to modernise their productive units (Silva, 1988).

The new authorities have shown no intention of repoliticising

the peasant movement or of intervening directly in labour conflicts between agricultural workers and their employers. There
are also signs that the agrarian entrepreneurs are beginning to
abandon their old belief that the state constitutes their 'natural
enemy', always ready to attack their interests. Recent events
show that the new democratic government looks at the difficulties being faced by the agrarian entrepreneurs, not merely as
private and sectoral problems, but as *national* ones. For example,
after close consultation with representatives of agrarian entrepreneurs, the Aylwin government came our in firm defence of fruit
producers against the adoption by the United States of protectionist measures affecting exports to that market. This official
commitment has been strengthened by the increased importance
acquired by exports of agricultural and forestry products.

The current continuity observed in economic policies with
regard to the previous government, has also eliminated many
fears among agrarian entrepreneurs. As President Aylwin categorically said in a speech to a conference on foreign investment:

> The democratic government does not want to go back to a
> state based pattern of development. On the contrary, the
> government will stimulate private initiative, interfering as
> little as possible with market decisions . . . Fortunately, the
> ideologization and polarization existing in the past in Chile on
> this matter have been overcome (*El Mercurio*, 23 May 1990).

In April 1990 the chairman of the *Sociedad Nacional de Agricultura*, Jorge Prado, made public his satisfaction with the continuation of free-market policies, stressing the 'mutual understanding'
existing in this respect between the landowner organisations and
the government (*El Mercurio*, 22 April 1990).

However, landowner organisations have also made public
their disagreement with the government decision to reform the
tax and labour laws. As a result of this, agrarian entrepreneurs
will have to pay higher taxes. In addition, the government
introduced among other measures new layoff regulations, intended to protect workers from unjustified dismissals. Nevertheless, the landowners' criticism has been carefully conducted by
their leaders, who have avoided any confrontation with the
government. This was clearly the case during Enagro '90, a
general meeting of agrarian entrepreneurs held in Santiago in

June 1990. With more than 400 delegates representing almost all the landowner organisations, this was the greatest entreprenurial meeting held in the country since 1980.

During the event, the Ministers of Agriculture and of Labour were invited to present the new agrarian policy and the forthcoming reforms. And, although they brought no 'good news', they received a warm and polite reception from the audience (see *Revista del Campo*, 2 July 1990). Landowners realise that these reforms are not aimed as hitting their specific interests, because they apply to all the sectors of the economy.

The agrarian entrepreneurs are also aware of the fact that the new labour regulations could contribute to maintaining social stability in the countryside, preventing the eruption of labour disputes and confrontation between workers and employers, which in the long run could be even more hazardous for their economic and political interests.

These reforms obtained broad support among the population and the major political forces in the country. In the post-authoritarian period, persons and institutions are extremely careful to prevent the adoption of positions which clearly antagonise those held by the majority. They do not want to be accused of having an anti-democratic bias. The landowner organisations know that if they become more explicit and militant in their criticism against the labour reforms, they risk again being labelled 'retrograde' and 'reactionary'.

During the 1980s the landowners' public image has experienced dramatic change. The transformations in the countryside have been accompanied by the adoption by agrarian entrepreneurs of sophisticated technology. They also have improved their managerial capability and modernised the marketing of their products. This, together with the export boom, has contributed to a substantial improvement in the agrarian entrepreneurs' image. In sharp contrast with the past, they represent today, for many Chileans, a symbol of modernisation and economic dynamism. The strengthening of the agrarian producers' public prestige, the acquisition of a more important position within the economy, together with the disappearance of the threat of land reform or the application of discriminatory policies, might constitute during the 1990s the basis for the achievement of a more stable and consensual relationship between agrarian entrepreneurs and the state.

References

Barraclough, S. and Fernández, J. A. (1974) *Diagnóstico de la Reforma Agraria Chilena* (Mexico: Siglo Veintiuno Editores).

Campero, G. (1984) *Los gremios empresariales en el período 1970–1981* (Santiago: ILET).

Carrière, J. (1980) *Landowners and Politics in Chile: a Study of the 'Sociedad Nacional de Agricultura', 1932–1970* (Amsterdam: CEDLA).

CIDA (Comité Interamericano de Desarrollo Agrícola) (1965) *Chile: tenencia de la tierra y desarrollo socio-económico del sector agrícola* (Santiago: Hispano Suiza).

Concertación (1989) Programa de Gobierno Concertación de Partidos por la Democracia (Santiago: Editora Jurídica Publiley Itda).

Echeñique, J. (1990) 'Las dos caras de la agricultura y las políticas posibles', *Proposiciones*, no. 18, pp. 145–58.

Gómez, S. (1972) *Los empresarios agrícolas* (Santiago: ICIRA).

Gómez, S. (1982) *Instituciones y procesos agrarios en Chile* (Santiago: FLACSO).

Gómez, S. and Echeñique, J. (1988) *La Agricultura Chilena: Las Dos Caras de la Modernización* (Santiago: FLACSO-Agraria).

Kay, C. (1978) 'Agrarian Reform and Class Struggle in Chile', *Latin American Perspectives*, vol. 3, no. 18, pp. 117–40.

Lehmann, D. (1974) 'Agrarian Reform in Chile, 1965–1972: an Essay in Contradictions', in D. Lehmann (ed.), *Agrarian Reform and Agrarian Reformism* (London: Faber & Faber), pp. 71–119.

O'Brien, P. (1981), 'The New Leviathan: the Chicago boys and the Chilean Regime 1973–1980', *IDS Bulletin*, vol. 13, no. 1 (December) pp. 38–50.

Silva, P. (1988) 'The State, Politics and Peasant Unions in Chile', *Journal of Latin American Studies*, vol. 20, no. 2 (November) pp. 433–52.

Vergara, P. (1985) *Auge y caída del neoliberalismo en Chile* (Santiago: FLACSO).

Wright, T. C. (1982) *Landowners and Reform in Chile: The Sociedad Nacional de Agricultura, 1919–1940* (Urbana: University of Illinois Press).

Zeitlin, M. and Ratcliff, R. E. (1986) *Landlords and Capitalists: The Dominant Class of Chile* (Englewood Cliffs, N.J.: Princeton University Press).

5 The Sugar Beet Industry: A Model for Agricultural Self-sufficiency in a Developing Country?
Robert N. Gwynne and Anna Bee

5.1 THE DISTORTIONS OF WORLD TRADE IN AGRICULTURAL PRODUCTS

Trade theory requires that production should be spatially concentrated in low-cost countries and that low-cost countries should export their production to high-cost ones. However, during the latter third of the twentieth century, the realities of global agricultural trade have turned this theoretical proposition on its head. Much of global agricultural trade is characterised rather by high-cost countries exporting high-cost agricultural products with high subsidies derived from either national or international administrations – for example, the US Federal Government or the European Community's Common Agricultural Policy.

The origins of such agricultural over-production in the developed countries can partly be traced back to a desire for self-sufficiency that emerged after the Second World War, linked to the belief that world food shortages would be a feature of the latter half of the twentieth century. As a result, European and North American governments decided to reduce the risk in agriculture by establishing fixed prices for food products at the beginning of the agricultural season. The farmer thus avoided having to deal with the uncertainties of the market at harvest or selling periods. By reducing the risk and making farming a safer business, these domestic price support programmes had an impressive impact on increasing agricultural production, created national and 'continental' self-sufficiency in Western Europe and soon caused the creation of huge food surpluses.

In order to 'solve' the problem of these surpluses, the governments of developed countries agreed to provide income in order to sell these surpluses off. Thus, on the world market, agricultural surpluses were sold off at a *fraction of their domestic prices*. As a result, a pattern of world trade has evolved that contradicts the principles of comparative advantage. Much of the world's food exports are now grown in industrial countries. Between 1961 and 1963 and 1982 and 1984, the industrial countries' share of world food exports increased from 46 to 63 per cent, while the share of the developing countries fell from 45 to 34 per cent (World Bank, 1986, p. 10). This has been particularly damaging for the export trade of those developing countries producing temperate-zone products (wheat, rice) or tropical products with a temperate competitor (sugar cane versus sugar beet).

There are therefore serious problems for developing countries attempting to expand agricultural production. On the one hand, international markets are increasingly restricted, either directly (through EC and US quotas on imports) or indirectly (through the cheap, subsidised exports of industrialised countries entering import markets). On the other hand, it can in the short term be cheaper for the developing country simply to import cheap, subsidised exports from Europe and North America. However, it is certain that if a developing country allows an untrammelled free market to regulate its agricultural economy, that economy may soon be suffering grave production decline as cheap, subsidised imports replace national production.

The agricultural problem for the developing country interested in expanding production can therefore be summarised as follows:

(1) How to expand production in sectors in which the country still has an international comparative advantage despite severe irregularities in the world trading system.
(2) How to develop some form of self-sufficiency in those agricultural sectors in which the present world trading system presents little possibility of a comparative advantage being realistically achieved.

It is to the latter problem that this chapter addresses itself. As with the developed countries, the developing country would be advised to reduce uncertainty in the agricultural economy and have fixed prices for farmers. However, unlike the developed countries, developing countries definitely do not have the resources to embark on massive (or even modest) subsidies if self-sufficiency were to change into surpluses. Thus, a scheme which year after year achieves approximate self-sufficiency without going into surplus is the best that the country can hope to achieve. This chapter will examine the problem of achieving such balance in the case of Chile's sugar beet sector.

5.2 THE WORLD SUGAR INDUSTRY AND CHILEAN SUGAR CONSUMPTION

Sugar and its very close substitutes, glucose sugar and high fructose corn syrup (HFCS), are derived mainly from three sources: sugar cane, sugar beet and high-starch products such as maize. Sugar cane was the earliest and cheapest source of sugar. Sugar production and trade in the EC has been one of the more extreme examples of trade distortion. Despite being a high-cost producer, the EC's share of world sugar exports rose from less than 9 per cent in the 1960s to more than 20 per cent in the 1980s, making the EC the world's largest exporter.

The world price of sugar fluctuated wildly during the 1970s. Due to major shortages, its real price trebled between 1972 and 1974. However, two years later, in 1976, it was back at its 1972 position, and subsequently declined even further. In 1979, the EC minimum 'interventionist' price for farmers was more than double the world price. However, the following year saw a brief resurgence of the world sugar price (when the EC price for once matched the world price) before again declining during the early 1980s.

During this time, the Chilean government had adopted a 'free trade' policy towards its sugar industry. During the late 1970s and early 1980s, it found that it could cheaply import sugar and did not seem to mind the run-down in its domestic sugar beet industry. As Figure 5.1 shows, sugar production from Chilean beet declined to less than 5 million quintals in 1980. One thriving industry at that time was the CRAV sugar refining factory in Viña del Mar. Because of the cheap international prices for crude sugar derived from cane, CRAV was able to import this crude sugar, refine it and sell it at lower prices than sugar derived from Chilean sugar beet. Thus, during 1980, more than 50 per cent of Chilean sugar consumption came from refined imports.

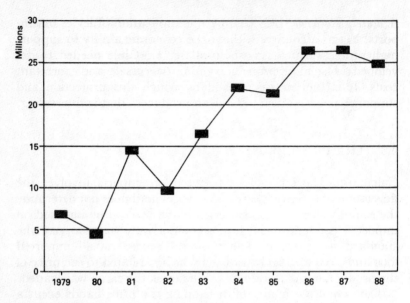

Figure 5.1   Sugar beet production, 1979–88, metric quintals

During 1981 and 1982, a serious debt crisis hit Chile and many of its leading companies, including CRAV. CRAV had been so profitable during the late 1970s that its owners had used it to generate funds for other ventures. By mid-1981, after only a year of high sugar prices, CRAV was declared bankrupt. The refining of crude sugar derived from cane came to an abrupt end.

However, refined sugar imports maintained their high levels and added to the trade deficit of 1981 and the more modest one of 1982. Trade deficits caused balance of payments deficits (due to large debt servicing obligations) and a new focus was placed on how to create a trading surplus and expand it. This had two elements − the expansion of exports and the substitution of imports. However, there was no wish to go back to the comprehensive import substitution seen in Chile prior to 1973 and only areas which were broadly competitive in international markets were encouraged and protected. One of these was sugar beet and sugar refining derived from domestic beet. Between 1982 and 1984, domestic sugar production more than doubled (see Figure 5.1); since 1986, national sugar beet production has come to supply the great majority of the national market.

The solution put forward in 1983 for the reduction of sugar imports was protection of the domestic producer, the *Industria*

Azucarera Nacional (IANSA), by the application of levies on imports. Yet as a country without the economic ability to support high protection in its agricultural sector, Chile needed to developed a system for protection without necessary and exorbitant costs. It is the precise method by which this protection and support has been given to Chilean producers that is interesting.

5.3 THE PRICE BAND POLICY

Calculating the tariff to be imposed on imports involves the development of a price band. The price band does not determine the selling price of sugar but simply the tariff to be imposed on imported products. The importers not only have to pay the standard 15 per cent tariff that is required on all imported foodstuffs, but also an extra tariff which is related to the price of the product on the world market the week the cargo was loaded.

The actual mechanics of developing the price bands occur a year in advance of their use. They are calculated in April each year, then published, coming into effect the following April. In the case of sugar the process of calculating the price band begins in March. In this month the average monthly prices for sugar on the international market over the previous 10 years are studied. These 120 prices incorporate adjustments for Chilean inflation. The prices are then arranged in descending order. The middle section of this list provides a more accurate representation of sugar prices over the previous years. The higher and lower prices, being extremes, are disregarded. Thus 35 per cent of the prices from the top of the list and 35 per cent from the bottom are removed, 42 figures from each end of the list. This leaves the 36 figures which were in the middle of the list. The lowest price that remains in the list will be the floor for the following year and the highest price will be the ceiling.[1]

5.4 SUGAR PRODUCTION IN CHILE

Sugar production is now solely controlled by IANSA. This company suffered during the free market years when the level of sugar production fell and large amounts of sugar were being imported from Argentina. Much of the Argentinian sugar was raw, and the importation and refining of this sugar was carried

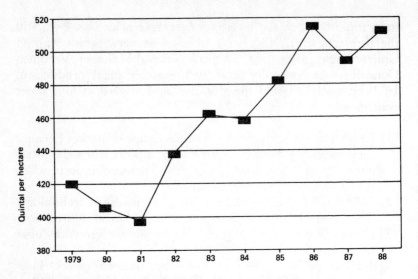

Figure 5.2   Sugar beet yields, 1979–88, quintals per hectare

out by CRAV. Sugar prices were not freed in 1974, instead CRAV received government subsidies to import and refine sugar (Mamalakis, 1976). At the same time IANSA received a high price for the sugar that it was producing, leading to a rapid and extremely unorganised expansion of sugar beet cultivation. In some cases only 3 tons were produced per hectare, compared with an average yield in 1986 of over 51 tons per hectare[2] (see Figure 5.2: 10 quintals are equivalent to one metric ton).

When sugar prices were finally liberalised in 1976, the Chilean market was flooded with cheap imports. Domestic production fell to its lowest level in years. By the end of the 1970s producers of sugar beet had little incentive to increase production because of cheap imports, a volatile world market and lack of technical knowledge and assistance.

Sugar production changed dramatically in 1982 because of the change in the national economic climate caused by the need to reduce the foreign debt. The increase in production was brought about by the policies first implemented by IANSA in 1982. The Pinochet regime intended to become self-sufficient in certain food staples by offering protection to domestic producers. Yet a price band policy was not initially introduced for sugar producers. Producers were offered guaranteed prices but were not protected from imports when the international sugar price was low. Still the directors at IANSA were able to be very positive about Chilean sugar production. The new General Manager, Verónica González, was especially active in promoting sugar production. In 1982, she evaluated the situation and arrived at four basic conclusions.[3]

(1) IANSA could not react to the international market because they could not compete with cheap imports when the international price was low or prevent expensive imports when the international price was high.

(2) Individual farmers could not afford to invest in technology. They needed financial assistance and technical information.

(3) Chile possesses good natural conditions for growing sugar beet.

(4) Internal producers cannot follow international prices. They need to be offered a price when they plant, not when they harvest.

With these arguments government support for IANSA came in the form of the '*Programa Remolacha*' (sugar beet programme) in 1982. The '*Programa Remolacha*' aimed to separate beet prices from sugar prices and offer the farmers a guaranteed price for their sugar beet when they planted. IANSA would then process the beet in its five factories and sell the sugar on the internal market.

In 1983–4 the real international sugar price was very low (Llandell Mills, 1984). IANSA would not have been able to finance the farmers indefinitely if the international price remained low, so once again government help was sought. The authorities added a special tariff on imported sugar of US$150 per tonne in an attempt to prevent the market again being flooded with cheap imports from countries such as Argentina. This was in addition to the standard 15 per cent tariff on all imported goods. It became clear that for the long term survival of IANSA, the government needed to step in and provide assistance. Thus in 1983–4 the price band policy for sugar was introduced. Figures 5.1–5.3 show how the level of production, the yields and the amount of land under sugar beet have increased. Production increased from 1 million tons in 1982 to 2.6 million in 1986 – since then it has stabilised, meeting national consumption

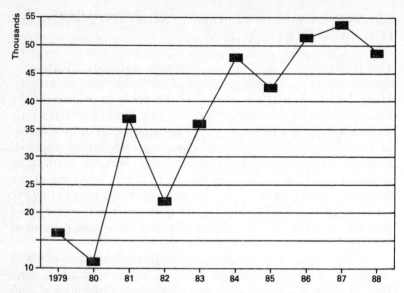

Figure 5.3   Land under sugar beet, 1979–88, thousand hectares

levels. Similarly, land under sugar beet increased from 22 000 hectares in 1982 to 51 000 hectares in 1986 – again since then stability has been noted.

The guaranteed beet prices offered to farmers are related to the price bands but are calculated in a different way and have been separated from the sugar prices since 1982. A supply curve for the beet is calculated for each sugar producing area, added to these are the expected yields and the distance to market. But all the farmers are paid the same price for their sugar beet except those in the Rapaco area. This area, which is the southernmost region of sugar beet cultivation, experiences less favourable climatic conditions than the other areas. The farmers are therefore paid US $3.00 extra per ton, as compensation for their higher costs.[4] IANSA has complete control over the amount of beet grown each year and this coupled with careful estimation of expected yields allows them to plan relatively accurately the amount of sugar to be processed the following year. This type of strict control over planting, and careful planning, allows a country without the financial means of supporting surplus production to maintain self sufficiency in sugar.

5.5 TECHNICAL AND FINANCIAL ASSISTANCE FOR FARMERS

The policies of IANSA could not have succeeded without a drastic improvement in yields and general efficiency of farmers. Many had received their land after the agrarian reforms of the 1960s and 1970s. The beneficiaries of this land often have only small holdings and little capital for improvements or investment in machinery. IANSA therefore began a scheme of financial assistance for each farmer growing sugar beet for them. The financial assistance came in the form of credit provided at the time of contract signing. With this the farmer was able to buy the seeds, fertiliser, products and services required for pest control and soil preparation. The farmer had to buy these provisions from the IANSA factory with which he was dealing.

Each farmer was also provided with detailed booklets explaining how to grow quality beet. The booklets were entitled, *Sugar Beet: A Guide to Its Cultivation* and *Sugar Beet: Preparation of Soils and Sowing, Irrigation and Drainage*. The first was the basic guide explaining in clear language how to grow the best quality beet by preparing the soil carefully, using the most suitable seeds and controlling pest. The farmers were expected to follow instructions in detail. The second booklet concentrated on the mechanical side of soil preparation, irrigation and drainage. It described the machinery which should be used. The machinery could be hired from IANSA, which proved important for the majority of farmers, who did not possess farm machinery themselves.

Much research has gone into the types of seeds, fertilisers and pesticides to be used. The policy of IANSA has been to ensure that the farmers can understand the information they receive and are given credit to obtain the required items. The farmers are supervised throughout the year by various IANSA officials. IANSA agronomists make regular visits to the farms in their area to monitor progress and to clarify any problems the farmers might have. IANSA attempts to be omnipresent throughout the sugar beet year. The import of capital and technology has had dramatic effects on sugar production per hectare. Not only have yields increased (from 400 quintals per hectare in 1981 to 540 quintals per hectare in 1989) but also the quality of the beet has risen. Although the minimum allowable sugar content is 14 per cent, the average in 1988 was 16.4 per cent.[5]

The technical and financial assistance provided to every farmer signing a contract with IANSA was a vital component in the increase in national production. Offering guaranteed prices provided the incentive the farmers needed to grow sugar beet; but with the provision of technical and financial assistance, yields grew by an average of 4 per cent a year during the 1980s. In Chile it has been shown that with a well planned system of incentives and technical aid, a relatively unorganised agricultural sector can show significant improvements. These improvements have helped the sugar industry in Chile to produce up to 8 tonnes of white sugar per hectare, which is more than the average of the EC or the United States (Llandell Mills, 1984).

5.6   THE ÑUBLE PLANT

Plant capacity

The Ñuble plant is one of the five plants presently operated by IANSA. It is situated in the Central Valley, a region which is subject to a classic Mediterranean climate of hot dry summers and mild wet winters. The average annual rainfall is approximately 760mm. The soils of this region are of volcanic origin and are very fertile, although they fix phosphorus, requiring large amounts of the mineral to be artificially added to the soil.[6]

The factory itself is situated 8km north of the nearest town, Chillán, on the Pan American Highway. The factory processes beet from the surrounding land; in 1988 over 11 000 hectares of beet were processed. In addition to the local beet, 790 hectares of beet from an area 270km to the south is transported by train to the Ñuble plant. Although this area is nearer the Los Angeles plant, the Ñuble plant has a greater capacity. The beet from this area is grown without the aid of irrigation, so the average yield is low, only 35 tons per hectare in 1988.

Since 1982 the daily capacity of the factory has increased from 3400 to 4880 tons. This increase has been brought about by better use of existing facilities in both the technical and organisation departments. It has been estimated that 10 per cent of the total cost of sugar production is accounted for by the actual refining process. Savings have been made, the most important of which has been in coal consumption. In 1987 the sugar yield was 87 per cent of the total possible amount that could have been produced from the amount of sugar beet delivered to the factory. The 13 per cent not extracted is lost in the process, for example 9 per cent is lost to molasses. Only minimal improvements could now be made in increasing the yield and the amount of investment needed would not be justified.[7]

The farmers at Ñuble

How have the policies of IANSA affected farmers? Interviews were carried out with farmers of the Ñuble region during the harvesting season of 1988. All the farmers viewed the policies favourably. There was a tendency for farmers possessing smaller properties, between 10 and 30 hectares, to be more appreciative of IANSA than the farmers with larger properties, of between 100 and 200 hectares. The farmers with smaller properties received a greater relative benefit from the technical and financial assistance than wealthier farmers with larger properties.

Few of the farmers interviewed owned any farm machinery. Most farm work is carried out by hand. The smaller farmers frequently have one or two family members working on the farm, while the larger landowners can afford to hire permanent staff. The seasonal demand for extra labour, during the harvest months of July and August and the thinning months of October and November, are met by hiring local labour. Most farmers possess one or two work horses. The low level of farm mechanisation makes the provision of machines by IANSA of vital importance.

The farmers have to pay for the transport of their beet to the processing plant, in either their own truck, one borrowed from a fellow farmer or one hired from a dealer in Chillán. IANSA pays an extra US $1.00 per ton per each 25km the farmer has to transport the beet beyond a 50km radius. The average distance between farm and plant was 32km and the greatest distance was 60km.

Without exception, the farmers growing sugar beet with IANSA have to sign a contract before planting. This contract is for the surface to be sown with beet rather than the tonnage produced at harvest. If the farmer sows more beet than was agreed in the contract, the surplus is bought at a considerably lower price. IANSA cannot afford to produce more beet than expected, so constraints such as these have to be placed on the farmers. Having signed the contract the farmers are provided with credit and technical assistance and most importantly a guaranteed price for the beet that they will produce in a year's time.

5.7 CONCLUSION

The rapid increase in sugar production in Chile since 1982 is impressive and bears testimony to what can be achieved with the implementation of suitable policies. Chile is now self-sufficient in sugar. The key to the success of IANSA's policies in improving efficiency has been the credit and technical aid given to all participating farmers. This allows even the least educated farmer with the smallest plot of land to produce high yields of beet. This illustrates how, given the incentive, plus a suitable form of aid, the peasant farmer can react rapidly and efficiently to produce a crop.

Government support is vital. If the debt crisis had not forced the government to reduce imports it is unlikely that protection would have been given to the producers of sugar, wheat and vegetable oils. Yet the policy of imposing variable tariffs on imports by the means of 'price bands' is now written as a constitutional law. This would make it difficult for any future government to refuse protection to domestic producers.

The policies that have been implemented in Chile and the effects they have had on sugar production could act as a model for other semi-industrialised countries seeking to increase food production. For the policies to be successful, though, it requires government involvement and support. It could be argued that the success of IANSA lies in the fact that it has an effective monopoly in sugar production. The fact that these policies have been implemented by a single agency has allowed IANSA to control the entire range of operations, from setting the beet price to arranging a contract with an individual farmer.

Notes

1. Information obtained during an interview with the Education Manager of IANSA, on 30 June 1988.
2. Interview, 30 June 1988.
3. Interview, 30 June 1988.
4. Information obtained during a second interview on 18 July 1988.
5. Information obtained during a visit to the Ñuble plant.
6. Information obtained from María-Eugenia Reyes, an Agronomist with IANSA.
7. Information obtained during an interview with the Production Manager at the Ñuble plant.

References

IANSA (1987a) 'Remolacha azucarera: Guía para su cultivo' (Santiago: IANSA).
IANSA (1987b) 'Remolacha: Preparación de Suelos y Siembra, Riego y Drenaje (Santiago: IANSA).
Llandell Mills (1984) *Revisión de la política azucarera chilena* (Santiago: Llandell Mills).
Mamalakis, M. (1976) *The Growth and Structure of the Chilean Economy: From Independence to Allende* (New Haven: Yale University Press).
World Bank (1986) *World Development Report 1986*, Part II, 'Trade and Pricing Policies in World Agriculture' (Oxford: Oxford University Press for The World Bank).

6 Non-traditional Agricultural and Agro-industrial Exports and Technological Change: A Microeconomic Approach

Carlo Pietrobelli[1]

6.1 INTRODUCTION

It is increasingly agreed that international trade plays a fundamental role in a country's development process. Moreover, it is important for a developing country to be able to diversify its exports, and become competitive also in manufacturing activities. This is also relevant for countries largely endowed with natural resources, like Chile, learning how to increase the value added of their productions.

Nevertheless, most of the available theories of international trade do not explain how comparative advantage evolves dynamically, and why. In addition, most of these theories have been developed for industrial countries, and miss out some special features of LDCs, whereas these countries strongly need and seize export growth and diversification.

Over the 1970s and 1980s Chile has been experiencing a remarkable export diversification, mainly towards natural resources (fresh fruit, wood and fish) but also in resource-based manufactures. Simple manufactures like foodstuffs, furniture, printed matter, garments and toys still account for a small share of the country's total exports (4–5 per cent), but their recent dynamism has been remarkable.

The aim of this chapter is to analyse the empirical evidence of some non-traditional exporters from Chile, making use of the results of a firm-level questionnaire carried out by the author.

Special attention is given to the agricultural and agro-industrial exporters in the sample, though they are not the only focus of the questionnaire. The eclectic theoretical framework adopted, briefly sketched in the next section, adapts some of the macro-economic theories of international trade to a firm-level concept of comparative advantage, and reinterprets trade theories in the light of some new ideas on micro-technology that apply to LDCs.[2]

6.2   THE THEORETICAL MODEL: TECHNOLOGY AND INTERNATIONAL TRADE THEORIES FOR LDCs

The rationale provided by the available theories of international trade does not satisfactorily explain some features of the recent international trade pattern.

For the present aims the received international trade theories are specially ineffective in explaining the evolution of comparative advantage (CA) over time. This is troublesome for LDCs, whose objective is a broader export diversification and the dynamic acquisition of CA in non-traditional activities.

The neoclassical (Heckscher–Ohlin) and Ricardian theories emphasise the benefits accruing to all participants in international trade, depending on the hypothesis of smooth and efficient functioning of all markets. In addition, their approach underlines the CA based on the present availability of resources, rather than its dynamic development that LDCs often pursue.

A possible remedy for some of these shortcomings may derive from a clearer understanding of technology and its evolution and international diffusion.

Many of the existing theories of international trade may still be useful, and provide a general eclectic theoretical framework in which to insert some concepts of technology more adequate to the 'imperfect' realities of LDCs. This may provide more powerful explanations of the dynamic creation of CA.

An assumption of the present study, which is supported by much empirical observation, is that CA does not only reflect the static endowment of given national resources. CA may result from explicit purposeful efforts to acquire 'technological capabilities' (TC), thereby adding to the country's endowments, and enhancing the effective utilisation of the endowments already available.

The inadequacy of the neoclassical approach for a more useful analysis of the technological dimension, especially in the context of developing countries, has already been noted in the literature.[3] More recently the analysis has moved long steps ahead, toward the building of a unitary theoretical *corpus* addressing the concept of technological change in LDCs.[4] As is well know by now, such an approach is centred around the concept of *technological progress* (Lall, 1990), that includes improvements in the ability to master a given technology and adapt it, minor innovations and major innovations. *Technological capabilities* (TC) are required to carry out all these improvements,[5] that are the result of purposeful, well-directed and costly efforts at the firm level, and imply lengthy learning processes (Bell, 1984; Stiglitz, 1987).

Two major drawbacks of most international trade theories is that they have been developed for the industrial countries, and have adopted a rigorously macroeconomic focus. On the contrary, this approach to technology for LDCs emphasises the relevance of the microeconomic dimension for the analysis of technical change. For my present aims, these theoretical developments are useful to add to the whole *corpus* of international trade theories, and help their useful reinterpretation in a dynamic perspective.

The idea of a dynamic evolution of the technological process and of continuous introduction of new products was already at the base of the 'technological gap' and 'product-cycle' theories.[6] They reject the neoclassical assumption of identical technology across countries for the same product, but miss out the complex process of learning and mastery and minor innovation which is necessary for efficient production, which can itself be a source of CA.[7] According to the 'product-cycle' theory, production is expected to move internationally following changes in technology. The new technology is expected to give exactly (and instantaneously) the same results in the buyer's and in the seller's country, as it is assumed that there is no other element to master after the new machinery and capital equipment are transferred. But actually the buyer and the seller do not share the same technological knowledge, and this brings about different industrial performances.

The need of costly and lengthy learning required in the process of assimilation, mastery and adaptation of the new technology is simply assumed away. Of course, the cost and length of learning falls with the level of industrial development, technological infrastructure and local TC; hence, it is probably higher in LDCs.

Taking into account the macroeconomic focus of these international trade theories, two important implications are derived.

First, technological change takes place continuously inside the firm, and it cannot simply be portrayed as a shift in the production possibility curve (*breakthrough*), as the neoclassical view would imply.[8] Different microeconomic performances are observable within the same industry. The difference in TC at the firm level (given uniform sectorial incentives and factor endowments) provides a firm-specific explanation of diverging performances and competitiveness.

Secondly, technological change requires purposeful, well-directed effort. It is neither only the automatic outcome of a repeated production activity ('learning by doing', *à la* Arrow, 1962), nor the result of abstract scientific research. It has to be actively seized and needs to be the object of an explicit entrepreneurial decision.

As a consequence, the use of *formal* technology inputs and outputs (e.g. the expenditure on R&D and the number of registered patents) as measures of technological innovation, although it is often the only possible alternative, underestimates the global amount of technological change actually occurring. In LDCs much technological change takes place through everyday experience at the shop-floor level, jointly with substantial efforts to assimilate and master the technology (Katz, 1984; 1987; Teitel, 1984).[9] Formal technology indicators miss out all these changes.

Given that *technological progress* is the relevant concept in this context, LDCs continuously experience technological changes. Thus, their CA can be explained by their relative advantage in any (or all) of the activities that range from the assimilation and mastery of the existing technology, to its adaptation and improvement, to breakthroughs in new production processes and new products. This is often a primary source of CA in LDCs.

To the extent that this form of CA depends on the disparity in countries productivity, it leads us to a 'Ricardian' explanation of international trade, in which *absolute advantages* in production determine the international trade pattern. This is consistent with an evolutionary approach to technology.[10] The absolute advantage is the outcome of a continuous, well-directed technological

effort at the firm level. Within this context, imported technologies can also provide a country with the opportunity to gain
a CA, if the capabilities to assimilate and master the new technologies are available locally, and if the government strategy is
conducive to this process. The human factor, and its different
specialised skills, is obviously crucial to carrying out this process
of continuous technical change.

Keesing (1966) has shown how the pattern of trade reflects
gaps in specialised skills and the dynamic dimension of their
creation across countries. But it is not clear what is the causal
theoretical link between human skills and internationally competitive activities. A detailed account of the relevance of human
skills in technology assimilation, mastery, adaptation, and improvement would help to this purpose. Such a process of continuous and purposefully seized technological change is the basis
for the acquisition of CA. The need for human skills is very high
throughout this whole process.

In this sense, also the *stages approach* to comparative advantage
(Balassa, 1979; Hirsch, 1977) can be interpreted as the result of a
gradual process of building and strengthening national technological capabilities (NTCs). This may explain why some countries
succeed in reaching higher stages, and others do not, depending
on the effectiveness of purposeful efforts and well-directed decisions to seize TC.

Another area of international trade theory that may be useful
to my purpose is represented by the theories emphasising demand factors in international trade (Linder, 1961). They provide
a radical alternative to the Ricardian and Heckscher–Ohlin
explanations, and underline the role played by countries' simi-
larities and the exchange of information between producers and
consumers.

According to these theories, the process of learning in manufacturing would take place only on the domestic market. Indeed,
this is often the case, but the possibility of a small country
specialising in a few varieties of a differentiated good demanded
in a specific foreign market cannot be ruled out. Of course, this
'learning' on the export market is not easy, and requires specially
skilled human resources and an adequate institutional framework providing access to the targeted market.

Access to the relevant information on a foreign market, the

ability of 'processing' this information to produce those goods with a large potential foreign demand, and finally the marketing skills needed to trade successfully, are all possible sources of CA. The availability of specialised 'marketing' or 'export' services is often a necessary condition to producing and trading internationally competitive goods.[11] Marketing and organisational skills can thus be independent sources of CA.[12]

Having outlined the eclectic theoretical framework that has been adopted, the *specific hypotheses* which are to be tested in the following section with the empirical microeconomic evidence are as follows:

(1) The firm is the relevant unit of analysis of comparative advantage. Inter-firm differences within the same sectors may be explained by a different capability to cope with and implement technological changes.

(2) The concept of *technological progress*, including technology mastery and minor and major innovations, has to be employed to analyse the role played by technology in shaping CA.

(3) Product innovation, through access to the relevant information on foreign markets, and adequate technical capabilities to 'translate' this information into new products, is an important potential source of CA for LDCs' firms.

(4) Information on the product/process technology and on the market does not flow freely and costlessly. A continuous and early transfer of information can be eased and made possible by specialised agents and institutions, and be the source of a competitive edge internationally.

(5) Formal R&D carried out in laboratories is important but, especially in LDCs, the bulk of technological change takes place inside the firm and is complementary and not exogenous to the production activity.

(6) Specialised and advanced human skills are crucial in order to perform all these functions of technological change, information gathering, processing, and deploying for production activities.

6.3 EMPIRICAL EVIDENCE: A CASE STUDY OF SELECTED NON-TRADITIONAL EXPORTS FROM CHILE

In Chile the period from 1970 to the present day has been marked by a clear tendency toward export growth and diversification (Table 6.1).

There has been diversification in products, in markets and in producers. The share of copper and mining exports over total exports has fallen from 86 per cent in 1970 to 54 per cent in 1987. A relatively small number of items makes for these changes, including fresh fruit (especially grapes and apples), cellulose, timber, fish-meal, and fresh fish, but this number is larger than in the past (Table 6.2).[13] A geographical diversification of exports has also been recorded (Table 6.3), especially towards the USA and Taiwan, South Korea and China (Gwynne, 1989). Furthermore, the number of exporters has increased in recent years.

To aid the analysis, between September 1988 and January 1989 I carried out a questionnaire on a sample of 26 'non-traditional' exporters. 8 of them are agricultural and agro-industrial producers. In each firm the owner, the general manager or the export manager, or sometimes all of them have been interviewed personally for 2 to 3 hours, in order to capture quantitative evidence as well as important qualitative aspects necessary to assess technological factors.

The sample is made up of firms of different size.[14] The agricultural and agro-industrial exporters are among the largest firms (Table 6.5). Most of the firms in the larger sample are fully owned by Chilean capital, with only 4 exceptions. An important discriminating criterion has been that all firms had to have *some relevant* export experience and undertake the whole export process, from production to sale on the export market. Hence producers selling their goods to trading companies taking care of all the export process, as well as pure 'traders' have been excluded.

However, it is always controversial what should be defined as 'non-traditional'. The definition obviously depends on the country and the time period considered. For Chile there is no clear agreement among authors.[15] It is true that the largest export products in 1970 are still leading the ranking twenty years later (Ominami and Madrid, 1988). However, in these years a

Table 6.1 Exports, 1970–87 (million dollars)

ISIC		1970	1973	1974	1975	1976	1977	1978	1979	1980	1981	1982	1983	1984	1985	1986	1987
	TOTAL EXPORTS	1111.7	1305.5	2144.3	1552.1	2082.6	2190.9	2477.7	3894.2	4670.7	3906.3	3821.5	3835.5	3657.2	3823.0	4222.4	5102.0
1000	MINING	950.4	1190.6	1807.0	1075.4	1443.6	1403.2	1492.2	2384.7	2771.9	2261.3	2267.8	2296.6	1982.5	2345.4	2316.2	2745.7
	(% of total exports)	85.5	91.2	84.3	69.3	69.3	64.0	60.2	61.2	59.3	57.9	59.3	59.9	54.2	61.3	54.9	53.8
1100	copper	839.8	1025.6	1653.5	890.4	1246.5	1187.4	1271.4	1899.1	2152.5	1714.9	1731.4	1835.1	1584.4	1760.7	1771.0	2100.5
1200	iron	66.7	61.6	72.7	90.0	86.3	81.5	79.6	124.3	157.6	161.9	158.2	112.0	110.6	91.5	88.4	101.0
2000	AGRICULTURE, LIVESTOCK, FORESTRY AND FISHING	32.8	25.4	54.8	86.1	118.9	160.1	203.5	264.5	339.9	365.4	374.9	327.5	428.0	501.8	646.2	743.0
	(% of total exports)	3.0	1.9	2.6	5.5	5.7	7.3	8.2	6.8	7.3	9.4	9.8	8.5	11.7	13.1	15.3	14.6
2100	Agricultural	22.4	20.7	42.9	59.7	86.2	126.6	157.7	183.8	244.3	268.0	278.1	253.7	345.6	420.6	557.1	605.1
	Fresh fruit		14.2	18.4	37.7	52.8	63.6	101.0	123.1	168.7	198.5	232.8	220.5	291.5	355.7	476.8	527.2
	grapes		4.3						44.7	51.8	76.0	107.7	125.8	164.7	215.5	249.0	275.7
	apples		6.4						43.1	74.7	81.5	81.8	62.9	74.5	74.3	126.4	141.9
	pears		1.1						7.9	11.9	13.8	12.7	9.3	11.4	12.6	25.2	24.4
2200	Livestock	7.7	1.3	4.1	16.7	24.8	23.2	27.8	37.5	36.9	29.1	33.5	26.4	29.1	25.5	37.7	54.2
2300	Forestry	1.3	1.8	3.2	3.7	1.0	1.2	2.4	3.3	1.6	2.1	2.2	2.3	1.6	40.9	40.2	71.0
2400	Fishing	1.4	1.6	4.6	6.0	6.9	9.1	15.6	39.9	57.1	66.2	61.1	45.1	51.7	14.8	11.2	12.7
3100	fresh fish	0.0	0.0	0.0	0.0	0.7	1.9	6.8	28.3	41.1	52.0	46.9	31.9	36.8			
2420	algae	0.0	1.6	4.6	6.0	6.1	7.2	8.8	11.3	15.6	14.0	14.1	13.0	14.3	13.0	9.0	9.5
3000	INDUSTRIAL GOODS	128.5	89.5	282.5	390.6	520.1	627.6	782.0	1245.0	1558.9	1279.6	1178.8	1211.4	1246.7	975.8	1260.0	1613.3
	(% of total exports)	11.6	6.9	13.2	25.2	25.0	28.6	31.6	32.0	33.4	32.8	30.8	31.6	34.1	25.5	29.8	31.6
3100	Foodstuffs	28.7	21.7	49.4	101.8	110.0	169.1	186.0	272.8	375.7	326.0	365.8	423.9	406.8	488.5	602.7	739.9

Table 6.1 continued

	1970	1973	1974	1975	1976	1977	1978	1979	1980	1981	1982	1983	1984	1985	1986	1987
3110 fresh fish														58.8	68.7	111.7
3198 fishmeal	1.8	12.2	31.2	29.2	61.1	86.1	105.8	152.6	233.7	202.0	256.0	307.1	275.7	314.3	333.2	358.3
3200 Beverages		2.6	4.1	3.9	7.0	7.9	9.8	27.8	21.4	16.7	13.1	10.8	13.6	20.4	21.5	33.5
3300 Timber	8.9	4.4	12.6	25.2	29.3	70.4	94.4	164.7	286.2	163.4	122.3	116.4	116.3	73.4	98.4	151.5
3320 simply wrought wood													74.3	51.4	69.0	
3400 Paper, cellulose and by-prod.	33.3	32.7	115.1	93.7	135.9	134.4	159.1	238.8	297.2	254.3	219.6	208.0	259.4	210.4	272.4	364.9
3410 paper		6.8	25.6	25.8	33.1	33.6	28.1	32.3	34.6	24.7	26.7	33.9	39.8	52.6	51.8	61.0
3420 cellulose		21.6	80.4	57.9	88.3	85.5	116.1	181.3	230.6	203.7	172.8	156.7	196.0	140.5	192.6	264.9
3500 Chemical & petroleum der.	10.9	6.9	42.0	46.4	64.6	77.9	106.2	128.2	163.2	148.2	139.9	109.8	123.8	79.9	84.3	103.3
3600 Basic metal manufactures	24.0	6.5	21.4	58.6	94.9	103.2	143.4	306.5	279.0	230.2	244.9	284.5	244.3	60.4	77.2	87.3
3640 copper		2.8	12.4	2.6	35.1	45.4	46.1	54.2	63.1	39.4	27.6	23.4	27.3	20.4	24.0	33.6
3700 Metal prod., machinery, elec.	7.7	4.6	9.7	42.4	52.6	36.6	56.5	59.5	63.9	43.8	35.8	20.3	19.5	13.3	23.1	26.8
3800 Transport equipment	5.3	3.4	5.3	7.0	4.9	11.3	8.1	26.0	42.9	74.1	22.7	29.0	42.1	17.2	53.7	32.2
3900 Other manufactures	7.9	6.7	22.9	11.6	20.9	16.8	18.5	20.7	29.4	22.9	14.7	8.7	20.9	12.3	26.7	73.9

Note: Data are classified according to a modified version of the ISIC, followed by the Central Bank of Chile. These are data on export 'shipments', which approximate the value of the goods at the time they cross the national border. Therefore these values do not necessarily correspond to the final actual values of goods sold abroad, which are relevant for the trade account of the balance of payments.

Source: Central Bank of Chile.

Table 6.2 Export product diversification, 1970–85, % of total exports of each year

SITC item		1970	1975	1980	1985
0311	Fish fresh	0.1	0.1	0.8	1.3
0320	Fish tinned	0.2	0.5	0.5	1.1
0514	Apples fresh	0.3	0.9	1.4	1.8
0515	Grapes fresh	0.3	0.8	0.9	4.9
0519	Oth. fresh fruit	0.3	0.3	0.5	1.5
0542	Leg. & veget. dry	0.4	0.7	1.0	1.0
0814	Meat & fish meal	1.3	1.5	4.9	7.6
2422	Saw-veneer-logs	0.0	0.0	1.5	1.3
2432	Lumber shaped	0.5	1.2	2.7	1.1
2517	Wood pulp	1.3	3.5	4.2	4.0
2712	Nat. sodium nitrate	1.1	1.6	0.8	0.9
2813	Iron ores	5.8	5.2	3.4	1.8
2831	Copper ores	2.3	1.5	5.1	7.6
2839	Non-ferr. ores	0.1	0.0	1.0	3.3
4111	Oils of fish	0.2	0.2	0.8	1.0
6411	Newsprint paper	0.8	1.5	0.7	1.3
6811	Silver unworked	0.0	2.0	2.5	1.8
6821	Copper unworked	76.6	52.1	41.7	39.0
	Total	91.60	73.60	74.41	82.30
	Total exports (US$ 000 of each yr)	1233598	1695562	4666604	3737551

Note: These are the four-digit SITC items that have represented at least 1 per cent of total exports either in 1970 or in 1985.

Source: CEPAL, Data Bank on international trade.

large number of goods have been exported for the first time, and the range of export goods has clearly widened.

Some higher value added manufactured exports have emerged, and their dynamism, if not yet their absolute values, is noteworthy and promising (Table 6.4). Thereby, my sample included firms producing agro-industrial goods, furniture, textiles and garments, some mechanical goods and the tinned fish and shell-fish industry. For the rationale of the choice of these sectors, see Appendix (pp. 112–14). Here, I will focus on the agricultural and agro-industrial exporters of the sample.[16]

As it was pointed out before, the *aim of this chapter* is to assess the role played by technological factors in creating firm-level comparative advantage in non-traditional productions, with special attention to agricultural and agro-industrial activities.

Table 6.3   Export market diversification, 1970–87,
% of total exports of each year

Country	1970	1975	1980	1985	1987
USA	14.1	8.6	11.0	22.4	22.4
JAPAN	12.1	11.0	10.9	12.0	11.0
EEC	58.0	45.3	40.5	35.2	32.7
GERMANY	10.9	14.5	9.5	10.0	9.5
HOLLAND	15.2	5.4	8.9	3.7	3.2
ITALY	7.5	4.7	5.6	5.3	5.4
UK	12.5	8.1	5.8	7.3	6.2
5 LAT. AM. COUNTRIES	9.8	14.1	20.4	11.1	14.3
BRAZIL	2.0	5.8	9.8	5.6	6.8
ARGENTINA	6.4	3.9	6.0	2.3	3.4
TAIWAN	0.0	1.0	1.0	1.0	2.5
KOREA	0.1	0.3	1.5	2.4	2.1
CHINA POP. REP.	0.0	0.7	2.2	3.3	1.5
Total	94.0	81.0	87.5	87.4	86.6

Source: CEPAL Data Bank on international trade;
Central Bank of Chile for 1987.

Table 6.4   Some examples of emerging exports, 1984–8, 000 $US

ISIC	Item	1984	1985	1986	1987	1988
2131	asparagus fresh and refrig.	1383	2107	3555	4452	5183
2169	oth. fruit fresh (kiwi . . .)	906	1330	3152	9706	232
2164+92+9	various berries	1391	1753	4832	7444	8697
315	fruit prepared	15171	16221	27883	34194	n.a.
3173	apple juice	5379	4593	10725	13132	14403
3189	apples dried or dehydr.	629	2114	2968	2918	4870
3114	hakes fresh & froz.	n.a.	1662	33914	62520	85880
3115	pacific salmon	n.a.	5	3586	5436	19577
313	tinned fish & seafood	39643	41030	74972	109471	67600
3161+2	clams tinned	2722	3255	7644	11801	18500
3440	printed matter	4950	7148	17128	28934	11800
3639	iron/steel nail, spikes	133	83	1261	3514	2382
3900	Textiles total	n.a.	20026	34443	54154	51825
3982	clothing women cotton	60	385	529	3594	12737
3900	Ceramic products	323	846	2348	14034	15857
3900	Furniture	0	825	1665	4876	7856
3990	toys	0	28	181	1360	2469

Note: n.a. = not available.

Source: Banco Central de Chile, Dirección de operaciones.

Table 6.5   Basic features of the sample of non-traditional exporters, 1988

Firm	Main product	Age (years at end 1988)	Export activity (no. of years)	Ownership (L=local)	Turnover (000 $US)	Exports (000 $US)	Employment (permanent and temporary)
Agro-industry							
1 Canned fruit		44	10	L	22000	5500	90+700
2 Frozen fruit-veg.		10	5	L	2000	600	120+700
3 Dehydr. fruit-veg.		48	5	L	2000	2000	400+600
4 Tomato paste		13	13	100% U.K.	20500	8500	500+1500
Agriculture							
1 Apples-kiwi		33	33	L	35000	28000	200+1500
2 Grapes		35	33	L	76700	76700	400+1437
3 Berries		5	4	50% USA	2500	2500	40+1000
4 Mushroom-asparagus		19	13	L	550	550	200
Agriculture & Agro-industry					161250	124350	1990+7637
TOTAL SAMPLE					356900	220290	11509+7637
ISIC 300 (1987)					3331770		
TOTAL EXPORTS (1987)					4997598		

Source: Author's questionnaire.

However, it is worth emphasising that the Chilean export diversification of the last two decades, as it has been argued elsewhere,[17] is the outcome of long and complex historical and economic processes and, as such, it needs a multi-dimensional explanation. No simple unidirectional explanations can be called for, and a careful analysis of the interaction and effects of macroeconomic policies and firm-level factors is needed, and attempted elsewhere (Pietrobelli, 1991). Thus, timber and fresh fruit exports are neither only the result of the neo-liberal management of the economy after 1974, nor the necessary outcome of the long-term public policies already implemented in the 1960s (Cepal, 1986). Macroeconomic policies have generally followed an outward orientation (though with some ruptures and uncertainties), while industrial and technology policies were lacking, thereby hindering the development of more complex industrial activities and of their exports. Some administrative and institutional reforms importantly contributed to create more favourable structural conditions to export, but selective and temporary incentives to non-traditional exports were introduced only after 1984, showing a more flexible attitude towards export promotion policies.

Most of these firms started exporting after a previous experience on the local market. At a certain stage, they found more convenient to sell on export markets than locally, hence revealing a newly created (or previously not exploited) CA internationally. Analysing this phenomenon, I will argue that, in addition to resource endowments and large manpower availability, technological factors played an important role in determining such a dynamic evolution.

Another important warning is needed before examining some detailed micro-evidence.

Only the *successful exporters* have been picked out. This obviously introduces a *bias* in the analysis, because not every Chilean firm succeeded in exporting during these years. On the contrary, in this period of abrupt policy changes, structural transformations and changing external conditions, the rate of firm mortality was high, especially in some sectors (Corbo and Sánchez, 1986; Mizala, 1985). The successful exporters are, in a way, the last survivors of a harsh competitive selection. For the purpose of a social welfare evaluation, their undoubtedly successful performance should be balanced against the large social and economic costs, in terms of suffering, instability, widespread bankruptcies, low or useless capital accumulation and learning before quickly switching to other activities in times of uncertainty and changing economic incentives, low rates of employment and overall deindustrialisation.

Moreover, the sectors from which these firms have been selected account for a small, though rising, share of total exports, and we have no counterfactual evidence on the possible effects of alternative policies on export activity. Still, investigating successful experiences may help to single out the determinants of the acquisition of a competitive edge.

Of course the size of the subsample of agricultural and agro-industrial exporters is small, but it will be compared, when necessary, with the whole sample of 26 firms. According to the agricultural and agro-industrial producers, their major sources of CA are low labour and raw materials costs, counterseasonality relative to customers' markets (namely the USA and the EC), and high product quality. On the other hand, transport costs and protectionism are the major disadvantages. All these factors are clearly relevant, but I argue that some forms of technological

Table 6.6   Sources of capital goods and technology

| | Agriculture and agro-industry | | All sample |
	largest source no. of firms	2nd largest source no. of firms	largest source no. of firms
Local	1	4	2
Abroad	7	–	24
Total	8		26
Purchased abroad from:			
Germany	2		14
USA	4		12
Italy	4		9
Japan	–		4
Denmark	2		4
Brazil	1		2
Others	2		15

Source: Author's questionnaire.

change have been crucial in determining the positive export performance.

As was to be expected, most of the firms in the sample buy their capital goods and equipment from abroad (Table 6.6). This is not surprising, given Chile's small and insufficiently diversified production of manufactured goods, and it is a feature common to most LDCs, with shallow and fragmented industrial bases. Yet, half of the smaller sample also buy some locally produced equipment, mainly simple and used machines.

It has been argued in the theoretical section above that an important form of technological change is the necessary activity of adjustment of the capital equipment and its adaptation to local productive conditions. Technologies designed under different circumstances to suit the economic conditions prevailing in industrial countries cannot be simply transferred to the new location and perform the same functions with the same efficiency. Time and effort are needed. This does not seem to be strongly confirmed by the results in Table 6.7, but in 50 per cent of the whole sample *some* minor or major change was required to adjust the capital equipment to local conditions.

Table 6.7   Effort to adjust capital equipment to local conditions

	Agriculture and agro-industry no. of firms	All sample no. of firms
Major changes	1	3
Minor changes	2	10
No change	5	13
Total	8	26

Source: Author's questionnaire.

To this purpose, it is interesting to emphasise the case of an agro-industrial firm that, thanks to a substantial effort to adapt its capital equipment to its particular needs, and to deep knowledge of customers' needs, sold its technology to other local and foreign producers. They had imaginatively to 'invent' a continuous-flow freezing tunnel to achieve the highest energy and time savings. This imaginative adaptation resulted in a machine that has been sold to some US manufacturers.[18]

However, in general little effort has been exerted to adjust and adapt capital equipment to local conditions. This is possibly due to the kind of technology required for such production, that is relatively simple and easy to transfer, even if very advanced, (3/8 reckoned their technology to be at the 'world best' level). However, technological change does not necessarily imply changes in equipment. The answers to this question might underestimate the amount of TC actually occurring. Thus, in spite of their declared small effort to change and adapt capital equipment, 88 per cent (7/8) of the firms declared that their technology had undergone some changes recently. More interestingly, for 75 per cent (6/8) of the sample these changes had been the result of their export activity, and all agro-industrial exporters emphasised that learning had been possible through exporting.

What kind of technological changes have they experienced? These changes cover a wide range of technological complexity, but they are mainly related to product innovations such as quality improvements; increased number of product varieties (including early and late varieties); more regular flow of production over the year in order to counter the typical seasonality of

Table 6.8   Main reasons for technological changes

Changes in	Agriculture and agro-industry most important reason no. of firms	All sample most important reason no. of firms	2nd most important reason no. of firms
Production scale	2	8	1
Inputs availability	–	1	–
Prod. characteristics	4	12	3
Need of higher effic.	–	3	2
No answer	2	2	–
Total	8	26	

Source: Author's questionnaire.

these activities; varieties more resistant to transportation and different temperatures; quicker and more efficient freezing techniques (entire block frozen – EBF – continuous flow tunnel); adaptation to a larger scale and to a smaller number of lines of production.

This is consistent with the more frequently mentioned reasons for these changes (Table 6.8). For 50 per cent of the subsample 'changes in product characteristics' has been the single most important reason for technological change, followed by 'changes in production scale' (25 per cent). Very similar results apply to the larger sample. It would thus appear that product innovation, induced by the search for the right product specification required by the exigent export markets, has been the most important form of technological change undertaken.

This form of technological change would probably have been the most frequent and relevant to these activities anyway. However, available macroeconomic evidence (Pietrobelli, 1991) shows that the general macroenvironment in these years in Chile was not favourable to other more complex and demanding forms of technical change. The country had a low level of NTC, both lower than it could have had with different policies, given the existing endowments, and lower than other comparable countries. Moreover, it invested few resources to build on its NTC. In such a macro context, only this 'simpler' form of technical change, requiring lower technological knowledge and less (and less sophisticated) equipment was possible, and the choice was more or less inevitable.

Table 6.9   Differences between goods sold on the local
and the export market

No difference	Agriculture and agro-industry 2		All sample 9
	1st most imp. reason	*2nd most imp.* reason	*1st most imp.* reason
Differences in:			
a. design	1	1	10
b. size	1	–	4
c. packing	–	1	3
d. quality	4	2	6
Total	6		17

Source: Author's questionnaire.

An important amount of technical change in these sectors takes place in the interaction between the firm, its customers and other external experts. Thus, for example, agro-industrial firms continuously supervise product suppliers (small and medium rural dwellers) and provide seeds, fertilisers, credit, and technical advice with their own technical teams. Moreover, they often benefit from the advice of foreign customers and experts.

This is consistent with what was emphasised in the theoretical section above, that 'formal' R&D in laboratories and research centres is also important, but does not reveal most processes of technological change actually taking place at a firm level. All the firms in the sample declared strong links and frequent contacts with universities and independent research centres, from which they acquired a number of services, like specialised advice and studies. Moreover, most of them (5/8) have also their own R&D departments. The larger agricultural producers have especially strong departments (stronger than the rest of the sample firms), with instances of over 30 researchers employed. They have been carrying out research on fruit and vegetable varieties, fertilisers and agricultural techniques at very advanced levels for many years.

Table 6.9 shows that export goods and goods produced for the local market *are* different. Home and abroad are not two alternative outlets for the same production, simply chosen on the basis of price incentives or strategic considerations. 75 per cent (6/8) of the firms declared that there was a difference between the goods they sold on the two markets, mainly due to differences in quality (50 per cent), design and size. This is often necessary to fulfil the binding sanitary restrictions that apply in industrial countries' markets.

The choice of product design and quality is a technological function that is crucial for exports. The majority of the sample firms declared they had the special human skills demanded to perform this function, and design their export products with the required characteristics.

However, many of these firms also benefit from assistance supplied by other intermediate agents external to the firm. More specifically, 'foreign buyers' (i.e. importers, wholesalers, other productive firms, retail chains, etc.) are an important source of technical assistance, and supply advice on product design to 88 per cent (7/8) of the firms (Table 6.10). The assistance to 'production technology design and adaptation' is also mentioned by 50 per cent of the firms as the second most important form of assistance received, and advice on a specialised function such as 'packing' is also frequent.

It is interesting to emphasise how the foreign buyers' support to exporters is not limited to conventional commercial and distribution functions, and takes numerous different forms. Foreign buyers from industrial countries may supply essential advice and help to 'materialise' CA otherwise only 'diffuse' or 'potential'.

To summarise, from the evidence reported above it stands out

Table 6.10   The kind of assistance given by foreign buyers

	Agriculture and agro-industry		All sample	
	most imp. reason no. of firms	2nd most imp. reason no. of firms	most imp. reason no. of firms	2nd most imp. reason no. of firms
Product design	7	–	21	1
Adapt to export mkts	–	2	3	10
Technology design & adapt.	–	4	–	5
Packing	–	2	1	3
No assistance at all	1		1	–
Total	8		26	19

Source: Author's questionnaire.

clearly that the right definition of product characteristics, and of a number of other detailed microeconomic variables related to the product, plays a very relevant role and can be itself a determinant of a competitive edge internationally. To this end, an appropriate 'institutional support' may be crucial.

An interesting example of support to technology acquisition and absorption for agricultural and agro-industrial activities (especially berries and fresh salmon, and generally resource-based manufactures) is offered by Fundación Chile, a private non-profit organisation created in 1976 by the Chilean government and a large US multinational, each contributing 50 per cent of the US\$ 50 million of initial capital.

A typical activity of the Foundation is to implement innovative projects through business ventures that are then auctioned off to the market. In this way, the Foundation points out new activities to the market and reduces firms' transaction costs, risks and related negative externalities. A wide range of technical advice and support services is also provided.

The special attention that the sample firms pay to the product, its quality and characteristics, and to continuous updating and adaptation to changing demand conditions, is also reflected in two other related aspects, certification of exports and quality control (Table 6.11). All firms have a separate department in charge of quality control, often with numerous people employed. The organisation of some firms confirms the key role of this sector. Thus, in some instances the quality control department depends directly on the export department and the firm's central direction, and is independent of the production departments. Most firms (75 per cent) also certify their exports. This is traditional in the agricultural sector, where firms are organised to provide their own certification internally. In the agro-industrial sector foreign and local organisations operate, providing the necessary advice and a highly valued control. The fishing industry now also is beginning to have local institutions qualified to provide these essential services, and with adequate international credibility. Such institutions prove specially valuable for incipient exporters, and foster the necessary process of product adaptation and upgrading.

In order to carry out all the essential processes that involve technological change, specialised workers, product and process designers and engineers are required. It was not possible to

Table 6.11 Certification of exports*

	Agriculture and agro-industry *no.* *of firms*	*All sample* *no.* *of firms*
Certify exports (at least sometimes)	6	21
WHO certifies exports:		
a. Same firm	5	8
b. Local organisation	2	10
Cesmec	–	(5)
Fundación Chile	(2)	(4)
Sernap	–	(3)
c. Foreign organisation	4	9
SGS	(4)	(9)
A. Knight	(2)	(2)
d. Customers	–	3

Source: Author's questionnaire.
* Many firms choose to have multiple certification of their exports.

obtain detailed data on the workers employed by each firm and on their qualifications, and sometimes the figures obtained were misleading due to the typical seasonality of employment in some activities. However, the wage level relative to other competitors in the same market may be a proxy for the availability of human skills. According to many interviews, skilled workers are highly sought after in years of economic recovery and fast growth of new activities. It is reasonable to assume that the more specialised and capable workers are rewarded with higher wages. Looking at Table 6.12, 50 per cent of the firms declared they paid their workers higher wages than local competitors, and 38 per cent 'the same wages'. This is possibly an obvious answer that any manager would give, especially in times of political transition, but cross-checks and additional evidence supplied by different independent sources confirmed these results.

There is therefore some evidence that the exporting firms in the sample paid higher wages than their local competitors, and hence disposed of a more highly qualified manpower. Most firms would have made substantial training efforts in the years of economic depression (Corbo and Sánchez, 1986), but my sample does not strongly confirm this result. However, all sample firms provide an array of productivity premiums and production

Table 6.12 Assessment of own-labour cost relative to
local and foreign competitors

	Relative to local competitors (no. of firms)		Relative to foreign competitors (no. of firms)	
	Agric. and agro-ind.	*All sample*	*Agric. and agro-ind.*	*All sample*
Higher/much higher	4	14	–	1
Same level	3	8	1	1
Lower/much lower	–	1	6	22
Don't know	1	3	1	2
Total	8	26	8	26

Source: Author's questionnaire.

bonuses, and in most cases (7/8) they employ personnel specialised in international trade.

However 6 out of 8 firms (22/26) recognised that they paid
'lower' or 'much lower' wages than their foreign competitors:
the lower labour cost had been a clear advantage for export
activities.

Finally, let us draw some conclusions from this overview of the
empirical microeconomic evidence presented.

6.4 CONCLUSIONS AND POLICY IMPLICATIONS

The main results of the analysis and their implications can be
briefly summarised.

Technological factors play an important role in exports at all
levels of technological complexity. The case of selected non-
traditional exporters from Chile empirically supports this
hypothesis for natural resource-based activities also, like agricultural and agro-industrial goods. In addition to good natural
resource endowments and low labour cost, technological progress explains firms' successful export performance.

However, technology has to be properly understood, and only
the broader concept of 'technological progress', that includes
technology mastery and adaptation, as well as minor and major
innovations, makes possible a better assessment of technological
dynamism in LDCs. In this sense, technology and learning also

have a role to play in apparently less technologically complex sectors, such as agriculture and agro-industry.

In the sample under analysis, technological change took the form of adaptation and changes in products, and especially product characteristics, colour, style, packing, sealing, and their constant adaptation to international demand requirements. This firm-level effort was often supported by the buyers (importers) themselves. Much attention has been increasingly paid to quality control and to export certification.

Some evidence also has been provided on the hypothesis that the firm is the appropriate unit of analysis of CA. Well-directed efforts along firm-specific learning curves have explained diverging export performances.

At the same time, however, macroeconomic policies, and generally the macro environment have to be conducive to exporting. The price incentives favourable to exports during most years after 1974 did not suffice to foster much technological progress other than product innovation. Industrial and technology policies were specially lacking. Long learning periods are required for more complex activities. Public policies did not help to overcome frequent technology market failures, and this may explain why technological progress took only the forms of product changes and adaptation. Yet further research is still needed on the link between these macro and micro determinants of export performance.

In addition, information plays a crucial role in explaining industrial and export performance. The relevant information is not easily transferred, and only at a cost. Specialised agents and institutions, such as trading companies, producer and exporter associations and 'foreign buyers' have eased the circulation of relevant information in this case, and sometimes they have even supported the process of learning and gradual acquisition of the capabilities needed to 'translate' this valuable information into exports.

Human skills and capacities are crucial to building CA in new activities. They are fundamental to carrying out any technological change, as well as to processing the information relevant to export. There is some evidence that the firms in the sample could dispose of highly skilled technical staff, and they generally paid higher wages and provided incentive premiums and bonuses to their workers.

What policy implications may one derive from the above analysis?

Briefly, public policies have two important roles to play. First, policies should be geared to overcoming technology market failures by supplying technical advice to individual firms. Such support to build supply-side conditions may foster the micro-economic learning processes that are necessary for the acquisition of CA and a good industrial performance. Export promotion policies should look carefully at the supply side and favour the acquisition of capabilities. Secondly, public policies have a place in fostering the acquisition of human skills, through adequate incentives to education and training.

Appendix: 'Questionnaire To Non-traditional Exporters, Carried Out by the Author in Chile, September 1988 – January 1989'

A questionnaire to 26 firms exporting non-traditional goods was carried out by the author in Chile from September 1988 to January 1989.

The main objective of the investigation was an attempt to assess the relevance of various factors for the building of dynamic comparative advantages in a developing country like Chile.

Particular attention was paid to technological factors (product and process technology), access to information on international markets, marketing and distribution strategies and institutional dimensions.

In each firm the owner, the general manager or the export manager was interviewed personally by the author for one to three hours following the questionnaire enclosed as a guideline for the interview.

The following criteria were followed to select sectors and firms in the sample:

1. Criteria to select the sectors
The selection of sectors was based on the observed evidence of recent export dynamism and on the absence/existence of some of the following characteristics, in order to have a relatively balanced and representative sample:

(a) Type of learning process
Group 1: sectors producing first for the local market, and 'learning' through a constant experience therein (FUR, SOFT, TEX, PRINT, MEC).
Group 2: sectors producing for the export market from the beginning (FISH, AGR).

(b) Impact of liberalisation:
Group 1: sectors highly dependent on international markets in terms of both

imported inputs and strong competition with foreign producers in local and foreign markets (TEX, MEC, PRINT).
Group 2: sectors less dependent on international markets (AGR, A.IND, FUR, FISH, SOFT).

(c) *Natural resource intensity*
Group 1: natural resources account for a high share of the value of final output (AGR, A.IND, FUR, FISH)
Group 2: natural resources are only the base for adding value to the final product and exporting it (TEX, MAN, PRINT, SOFT).

(d) *Labour intensity*
Group 1: high relevance of labour cost in the production process (AGR, FUR, FISH, PRINT, TEX).
Group 2: low relevance of labour costs (MEC, A.IND, SOFT).

2. Criteria to select the firms
Firms were selected:
1. having some exporting experience (at least 2–3 years);
2. of differing dimensions (some small, some large);
3. experiencing the whole export process, from production to sale on the international market. Hence producers selling their goods to trading companies yet uninterested or avoiding the international market have been excluded.
The inclusion of *Multinational Companies* (MNCs) in the sample *was not a discriminating criterion*, although it could probably have provided different explanations of the exporters' performance.
    The final selection was restricted by access to interviews, so that some firms had regrettably to be excluded, such as some toys' manufacturers and other mechanical producers.
    Ultimately, the following sectors were selected (number of firms in parentheses):

– Agro-industry (4)	A.IND
– Fresh fruit (4)	AGR
– Furniture (4)	FUR
– Textiles and clothing (4)	TEX
– Fish (and canned fish) (4)	FISH
– Mechanical (4)	MEC
– Others (2)	VAR
– + Software (1)	SOFT
– + Printing (1)	PRINT
Total number of firms	26

Moreover, *interviews* with the following agents and institutions were conducted:

– Prochile
– Fundación Chile
– Ministerio de Economía, Dep. de comercio exterior

– Banco Central, Dep. técnico de comercio exterior
– Asociación de Exportadores de Chile
– Asexma,
– Asimad,
– Asociación de Exportadores de Salmones y Trucha
– Primex, private US trading company based in Chile

Notes

1. I wish to thank R. Thorp, S. Lall, A. Aninat, F. Fajnzylber, R. Ffrench-Davis, and all the participants to the Annual Conference of the Society for Latin American Studies, Jesus College, Oxford (March 1990), where a preliminary version of this paper was presented. However, the responsibility for errors and omissions is mine.
2. For a detailed discussion of the theoretical framework, only briefly reviewed here, see Pietrobelli (1991).
3. See Stewart (1977) and the classic work of Nelson and Winter (1982) among many.
4. Basic references on the concept of technological change in LDCs are: Dahlman *et al.* (1987); Fransman and King (1984); Katz (1984); Lall (1987; 1990); Pack and Westphal (1986).
5. Obviously, many other capabilities are required to manage an industrial activity efficiently over time, such as entrepreneurial and managerial capabilities. Still, TC are crucial, because firms and countries need them to benefit from technical knowledge (Katz, 1984).
6. See Posner (1961); Vernon (1966); Hufbauer (1970); Hirsch (1967).
7. In a broader sense, this idea of learning and mastery also applies to all the managerial and administrative processes that are required for efficient production and export.
8. Simon Teitel emphasises that technological change is complementary to the production activity, and that 'it should be conceptualized as a necessary answer to the presence of constraints and bottlenecks that must be bypassed or removed to accomplish production' (Teitel, 1984, p. 58).
9. Yet economic historians have also shown how in industrial countries part of the productivity increases has been derived from small improvements and adaptations rather than major innovations and breakthroughs (Rosenberg, 1976).
10. See Dosi and Soete (1988; 1983). In their theoretical framework: 'international technological asymmetries (i.e. absolute advantages) define the *boundaries of the universe* within which cost-based (and, *in primis*, wage based) adjustments can take place' (Dosi and Soete, 1983, p. 203).
11. In this context, an interesting new line of research is stressing the relationship between new exporters of light manufactured goods from LDCs and 'foreign buyers' from industrial countries, that provide specialised services to the LDCs' manufacturers and help them to gain access to the industrial countries' markets.
12. Such search for information and investment in TC building may help

LDCs to catch up industrial countries in some specialised activities, in sectors that are experiencing smaller shifts in the international technology frontier, and in the phases of introduction and maturity of a technology's life (Perez and Soete, 1988).

13. Changes in the Central Bank's criteria of export classification complicate the interpretation of the data. For example, in 1985 fresh fish was moved from the 'agricultural, livestock and seafood' subgroup to the 'industrial' one. Fish-meal, a relatively low value added commodity, is still considered 'industrial', and accounted for 22.2 per cent of total industrial exports in 1987. This also occurs with timber.

14. With total turnover and exports ranging from US$ 77 million to only 0.3 million, and average values of US$ 13.7 million and 8.4 million respectively.

15. See Ffrench-Davis (1987); Ominami and Madrid (1988); Ossa (1988).

16. Being 'agro-industry' and 'agriculture' composite items, it is not easy to derive separate figures from the official data. The External Trade Department of the Banco Central de Chile estimated that the export shippings of agricultural and agro-industrial goods have been respectively: US$ (000) 363 851 and 44 330 in 1985; 489 029 and 73 828 in 1986; 546 079 and 99 315 in 1987. Rapid growth is clear from these figures.

17. For detailed analyses of the various determinants of Chilean export diversification, see my 1989 ECLA paper and D.Phil. dissertation (1991).

18. A similar case of 'technology' export is that provided by the large software exporter in the sample (of a package for banking services).

References

Arrow, K. J. (1962), 'The Economic Implications of Learning by Doing', *Review of Economic Studies*, vol. 29, pp. 155–73.

Balassa, B. (1979) 'A "Stages Approach" to Comparative Advantage', in I. Adelman (ed.), *Economic Growth and Resources, vol. 4, National and International Policies* (London: Macmillan-IEA).

Bell, M. (1984) '"Learning" and the Accumulation of Industrial Technological Capacity in Developing Countries', in Fransman and King (1984).

Cepal, (1986) *El desarrollo frutícola y forestal en Chile y sus derivaciones sociales*, Estudios e Informes de la Cepal, no. 57 (Santiago: UN).

Corbo, V. and Sánchez, J. M. (1986) 'Adjustments by Industrial Firms in Chile during 1974–82', in V. Corbo *et. al.*, *World Bank Working Paper, no. 764* (Washington, D.C.: World Bank).

Dahlman, C., Ross-Larson, B. and Westphal, L. E. (1987) 'Managing Technological Development: Lessons from Newly Industrializing Countries', *World Development* (June).

Dosi, G. and Soete, L. (1983) 'Technology Gaps and Cost-based Adjustment: Some Explorations on the Determinants of International Competitiveness', *Metroeconomica*, vol. 35, pp. 197–222.

Dosi, G. and Soete, L. (1988) 'Technical Change and International Trade', in G. Dosi, C. Freeman, R. Nelson, G. Silverberg and L. Soete (eds) *Technical Change and Economic Theory* (London: Pinter Publishers) pp. 401–31.

Ffrench-Davis, R., (1987) 'Políticas Comerciales en Chile, 1973–86', *CIEPLAN* (Santiago) (May) (mimeo).

Fransman, M. and King, K. (eds) (1984) *Technological Capability in the Third World* (London: Macmillan).

Gwynne, R. N. (1989) 'Third World Industrialization and the Pacific Rim: Contrasts in Trade Orientation and the Implications for Chile', paper presented at the *General Symposium of the Pacific Science Association*, VI International Congress (Valparaiso) (August).

Hirsch, S. (1967) *Location of Industry and International Competitiveness* (Oxford: Clarendon Press).

Hirsch, S. (1977) *Rich Man's, Poor Man's and Everyman's Goods: Aspects of Industrialisation* (Tübingen: J. C. B. Mohr).

Hufbauer, G. C. (1970) 'The Impact of National Characteristics and Technology on the Commodity Composition of Trade in Manufactured Goods', in R. Vernon, *The Technology Factor in International Trade* (New York: NBER).

Katz, J. (1984) 'Domestic Technological Innovations and Dynamic Comparative Advantage', *Journal of Development Economics*, vol. 16, nos. 1–2, pp. 13–38.

Katz, J. (ed.) (1987) *Technology Generation in Latin American Manufacturing Industry* (London: Macmillan).

Keesing, D. B. (1966) 'Labor Skills and Comparative Advantage', *American Economic Review*, vol. 56, pp. 249–58.

Lall, S. (1987) *Learning to Industrialize: The Acquisition of Technological Capability by India* (London: Macmillan).

Lall, S. (1990) *Building Industrial Competitiveness: New Technologies and Capabilities in Developing Countries* (Paris: OECD Development Centre).

Linder, S. B. (1961) *An Essay on Trade and Transformation* (New York: Wiley).

Mizala, A. (1985) 'Liberalización financiera y quiebra de empresas industriales: Chile, 1977–82', *Notas Técnicas CIEPLAN*, no. 67 (January).

Nelson, R. R. and Winter, S. G. (1982) *An Evolutionary Theory of Economic Change* (Cambridge, Mass.: Harvard University Press).

Ominami, C. and Madrid, R. (1988) *Lineamientos estratégicos para una inserción activa en los mercados internacionales*, Instituto Latinoamericano de Estudios Internacionales (Santiago: ILET).

Ossa, F. (1988) 'Políticas de fomento al sector exportador chileno', *Documenso de Trabajo, no. 114, Univ.Católica de Chile* (Santiago) (November).

Pack, H. and Westphal, L. E. (1986) 'Industrial Strategy and Technological Change', *Journal of Development Economics*, vol. 22, pp. 87–128.

Perez, C. and Soete, L. (1988) 'Catching up in Technology: Entry Barriers and Windows of Opportunity', in G. Dosi, C. Freeman, R. Nelson, G. Silverberg and L. Soete (eds), *Technical Change and Economic Theory* (London: Pinters Publishers) pp. 458–79.

Pietrobelli, C. (1989) 'The Process of Export Diversification in Chile, 1960–88', *ECLA/UNIDO Division of Industry and Technology* (Santiago) (March).

Pietrobelli, C. (1991) *Dynamic Comparative Advantage, Local Technological Capability and Manufactured Exports: the Case of Chile since 1973*, D.Phil. dissertation (University of Oxford).

Posner, M. V. (1961) 'International Trade and Technical Change', *Oxford Economic Papers*, vol. 13, pp. 323–41.

Rosenberg, N. (1976) *Perspectives on Technology* (Cambridge: Cambridge University Press).

Stewart, F. (1977) *Technology and Underdevelopment* (London: Macmillan).

Stiglitz, J. E. (1987) 'Learning to Learn, Localized Learning and Technical Progress', in P. Dasgupta and P. Stoneman (eds), *Economic Policy and Technological Development* (Cambridge: Cambridge University Press).

Teitel, S. (1984) 'Technology Creation in Semi-industrial Economies', *Journal of Development Economics*, vol. 16, pp. 39–61.

Vernon, R. (1966) 'International Investment and International Trade in the Product-cycle', *Quarterly Journal of Economics*, vol. 80, pp. 190–207.

7 Rural Credit, Agricultural Extension and Poverty Alleviation: Past Experience and Future Perspectives

Christopher D. Scott[1]

7.1 INTRODUCTION

After 17 years of military dictatorship characterised by a preoccupation with microeconomic efficiency and macroeconomic stabilisation, the alleviation of poverty has once again become a political priority in Chile. This chapter attempts to contribute to the current debate on anti-poverty strategies by reviewing the experience of selected policies targeted at small farmers from the 1960s to the 1980s.

The chapter is divided into three parts. The first (section 7.2) reviews the evidence on changes in the extent and nature of rural poverty in Chile since 1970. The second (section 7.3) provides a limited assessment of programmes of rural credit and agricultural extension undertaken by the Institute of Agricultural Development (INDAP). This section is based on material from a panel study of rural households interviewed in 1968 and 1986. The third (section 7.4) discusses some proposals for alleviating poverty in small holding communities which might form part of an overall strategy of rural development for the 1990s.

7.2 THE EVOLUTION OF POVERTY SINCE 1970

Since Chile is a highly urban society, it will be of value to review the evolution of poverty in the country as a whole before examining the nature of rural poverty in more detail.

Trends in aggregate poverty

Unfortunately, it is impossible to establish with any precision how the incidence of absolute poverty has changed since 1970, owing to a lack of reliable and consistent time series data. Two sets of studies offer poverty estimates for the period 1970–80, but both are subject to severe methodological weaknesses.

The United Nations Economic Commission for Latin America (ECLAC) calculated headcount measures of poverty for 10 Latin American countries in 1970 (ECLAC, 1985). In order to define the poverty line, ECLAC estimated the money income required to purchase a food basket which met the minimum energy and protein requirements recommended by FAO/WHO. This was termed the 'destitution level of income'.

Since household survey data indicated that urban families spending just over the level required to purchase the minimum food basket allocated between 40–50 per cent of their total expenditure to food, the urban poverty line was drawn at twice the destitution level of income. The rural poverty line was set at 1.75 times the destitution level, because low income rural households assigned more than half their total expenditure to the purchase of food. Using this methodology, ECLAC estimated that in 1970 1.6 million Chileans (17 per cent of the population) were living in poverty and 0.6 million Chileans (6 per cent of the population) were destitute.

Projections for 1980 suggested that the number of poor had risen to 1.8 million, but the headcount ratio had declined to 16 per cent. However, these projections assumed that the average income of the poor had increased by 70 per cent of *per capita* income growth between 1970 and 1980, while the poverty line was raised by an amount equivalent to only one-quarter of the increase in *per capita* income over the same period. These assumptions seem overly optimistic.

The only source of consistent time series information on poverty incidence is provided by the Maps of Extreme Poverty which were drawn up on the basis of the Population and Housing Censuses of 1970 and 1982 (ODEPLAN-IEUC, 1975; 1986). In this case, the same methodology was employed in each year, so that the estimates are directly comparable. The difficulty lies with the definition of 'extreme poverty', which was based on four criteria: (1) type of housing; (2) type of domestic sanitary system; (3) presence of overcrowding; and (4) possession of consumer durables.

No reference was made to household income or expenditure data, so the Maps are not identifying poverty as traditionally understood at all. Furthermore, the information contained in the Maps cannot even be interpreted as a partial index of basic needs fulfilment. This is because the possession of a single item, which may have only a tenuous connection with the satisfaction of basic needs, such as a radio, television or telephone was sufficient to place a household above the extreme poverty line (Raczynski, 1986; Ortega and Tironi, 1988, pp. 22–5).

The results of this mapping exercise suggest that in 1970, 1.9 million Chileans (21 per cent of the population) lived in poverty, while in 1982 the number of poor had declined to 1.5 million (14 per cent of the population). These figures are even more optimistic than the ECLAC projections because they indicate a decline not only in the headcount ratio, but also in the absolute number of poor during the 1970s.

Other poverty estimates resulting from the application of different methodologies exist for various reference periods after 1979. These estimates suggest that between 31 per cent and 45 per cent of the population was living in poverty by the mid-1980s (Table 7.1). It therefore seems most plausible to conclude that aggregate poverty increased substantially between 1970 and 1985. In terms of the headcount ratio, the extent of poverty more than doubled during this period.

Trends in rural poverty

The term 'rural poverty' is ambiguous. It could refer to the incidence of poverty among the population resident in rural areas, or to the number of poor among the population dependent on rural employment. In highly urbanised semi-industrial countries, where part of the agricultural sector is technically advanced, these two reference groups are by no means congruent, as is explained below. The sources used here define rural poverty with respect to the population resident in rural areas, which includes all settlements of less than 300 inhabitants.

Evidence on the evolution of rural poverty is more sparse, and the available estimates are less consistent than those for aggre-

Table 7.1 Estimates of poverty, 1970–85

Source	Reference period	Coverage	Aggregate poverty		Rural poverty		
			No. of poor[a]	% of pop.	No. of poor[a]	% of rural pop.	% of total poor
ECLAC	1970	National	1.6(P)	17	0.6(P)	25	38
ECLAC	1970	National	0.6(D)	6	0.35(D)	11	58
ECLAC	1980	National	1.8(P)	16	0.6(P)	27	33
Map of Ext. Pov.	1970	National	1.9	21	0.62	25	32
Map of Ext. Pov.	1982	National	1.5	14	0.39	20	25
ODEPLAN	1979	National		45			
ODEPLAN (CAS)	1982	National		c.40			
Rodríguez	1982	National		30(D)		55(D)	
Pollack–Uthoff	1984	Greater Santiago		48(P)			
Pollack–Uthoff	1984	Greater Santiago		23(D)			
ODEPLAN (CASEN)	1985 (Nov)	National		45(P)			
Torche	mid-1980s	National		45			
Vergara	mid-1980s	National		31			
Urzúa	1982	Rural				56	

Notes: [a] in millions.
(P) = poor (see text).
(D) = destitute (see text).

Sources: See References at end of Chapter.

gate poverty. The ECLAC projections suggest that the absolute number of rural poor remained unchanged during the 1970s, while the rural headcount ratio rose slightly from 25 per cent to 27 per cent. The Poverty Maps indicate a decline both in the incidence of extreme poverty in the rural areas and a fall in the headcount ratio from 25 per cent to 20 per cent.

By contrast, Urzúa (1984) who used the Altimir methodology which underlies ECLAC's poverty estimates for 1970, calculated that in 1982 the rural poor amounted to 1.2 million persons, or 56 per cent of the rural population. This figure is much more consistent with other corroborative evidence from the labour market, and suggests that the headcount ratio for rural poverty more than doubled during the 1970s. This rapid increase in rural impoverishment was the result of increased landlessness following the counter-reform of the Pinochet administration, rising unemployment and a sharp decline in real agricultural wages which fell by half between 1970 and 1979 (Jarvis, 1985, p. 63).

In summary, it appears that between 1970 and the economic crisis of 1982–3, the number of urban and rural poor increased and the aggregate headcount ratio more than doubled. Since 1983, the situation has improved following the decline in unemployment rates and the rise in real wages. Nevertheless, a substantial amount of poverty still exists in the country. Most of the poor are urban resident, but the proportion of the population living below the poverty line in the countryside is greater than that in the cities.

Changes in the composition of the rural poor

Not only did rural poverty increase sharply between 1970 and the mid-1980s, but the characteristics of the rural poor have changed in three significant ways over this period. First, an increasing proportion of poor households for whom rural employment was the primary source of income became located in urban or suburban settlements. A large number of permanent workers in agriculture lost their jobs when the agrarian producer co-operatives and agricultural trade unions were dissolved after 1973. These displaced labourers lost their homes as well as their jobs and were forced to migrate. The result of this migration was the creation of rural townships (*aldeas rurales*) which are now an established feature of the social landscape of agriculture (Rivera and Cruz, 1984).

Secondly, the number of permanent paid workers in agriculture declined by 20 per cent between 1965 and 1976 (de Janvry *et al.*, 1986, p. 65), while the main growth in agricultural employment since the mid-1970s has been for seasonal work, due to changes in the pattern of land use and selective mechanisation. This suggests that temporary wage labourers now constitute a larger proportion of poor households for whom rural employment is the main source of income.

Some of these temporary workers are ex-permanent labourers, but there is a younger generation in this labour supply whose only employment experience has been casual work in rural or

Table 7.2   Composition of household income in rural townships, 1982, %

Income Source	San Felipe Los Andes	Santiago	Molina	Ñuble	Osorno	Total
Temporary rural employ.	42.4	23.3	37.2	35.7	25.6	32.9
Permanent rural employ.	11.5	6.6	11.7	8.4	8.9	9.5
Temporary urban employ.	7.4	23.6	4.0	5.6	9.8	10.5
Permanent urban employ.	6.9	14.1	5.2	8.8	1.7	7.2
Share-cropping	3.5	3.7	1.8	5.4	0.3	2.7
Self-employment	0	8.6	0	0	5.7	3.1
Unemployment benefit	5.2	3.1	4.3	11.6	7.4	5.9
Emergency employ. prog	5.3	3.3	4.3	9.4	8.4	5.9
Pensions	11.0	8.0	16.0	5.3	19.9	12.5
Soc. sec. contribs	4.1	4.6	10.4	5.2	9.0	6.6
Child allowances	2.7	1.1	5.1	4.6	3.3	3.2
Total	100	100	100	100	100	100
No. of households	71	45	75	53	87	331

Source: Rivera and Cruz (1984) Table 55, p. 186.

urban labour markets (Gómez, 1987, p. 200). Nevertheless, despite the greater variance in monthly labour requirements per hectare of export crops compared to traditional crops, off-peak labour demand per hectare for apples and peaches is greater than peak labour demand per hectare for crops such as wheat, potatoes and milk (Valdés, 1988, p. 404).

Thirdly, the sources of household income among the poor have changed. In part, this is a direct consequence of the 'urbanisation–casualisation' of the agricultural labour force. Urban residence offers the possibility of some casual employment outside of agriculture, while the increasingly seasonal nature of agricultural labour demand forces '*pobladores rurales*' to seek non-agricultural jobs at certain times of year (Table 7.2).

However, it is not at all clear that these processes have led to a more diverse portfolio of income sources among the poor than in the past. In the mid-1960s, most *inquilinos* in the Central Valley received a real wage made up of a cash payment; access to a plot to grow food crops for self-consumption; a right to pasture some large animals on estate land and to keep small livestock in the domestic compound; tied housing (together with such services as drinking water); and employers' social security contributions (Ramírez, 1968; Valdés, 1971).

While the quality of housing provided was often deplorable, and some employers evaded the payment of social security contributions, the real incomes of these workers came from a variety of sources within the estate. In contrast, temporary employment contracts currently used in the Central Valley have narrowed these entitlements to a single cash wage, while the possibilities for keeping small livestock and producing food crops on urban plots in the rural townships are much diminished (Derksen, 1990, p. 173).[2]

Environmental degradation has also reduced the variety of income sources available to the poor in some rural areas. In many communities in the Norte Chico, the production of charcoal and the sale of firewood is now prohibited. Deforestation in *minifundio* communities located in the coastal range in Southern Chile has reduced the opportunity for hunting game. Wildfowl stocks have declined in Lake Budi, which is close to some of the poorest Mapuche settlements, and the salination of the lake's water supply following the earthquake in 1961 has reduced its fish stocks.[3] The intensity of marine exploitation in the inshore coastal areas of Llanquihue and Chiloé in recent years may also have reduced the opportunities for poor households to supplement their incomes by collecting shell fish and sea weed.[4] Nevertheless, in long-established rural communities, considerable diversity of income sources persists among poor households (de los Reyes, 1990, p. 149).

Changes in government policy towards the poor in the last 20 years have also affected the relative significance of particular income sources among low income households. During the 1960s, the Frei administration's strategy of rural development included land reform, the promotion of labour unions, the implementation of effective minimum wages, the provision of subsidised credit and agricultural extension to small farmers and increased welfare coverage (state transfers, health and education) of the rural population.

By the mid-1980s, no further redistribution of land was contemplated either by the Pinochet government or the Christian Democrat opposition, labour unions had been dissolved, the small farmer credit programme had been scaled down and refocused, and agricultural extension was privatised. In contrast, wage income from the emergency 'workfare' programmes, such as the PEM and POJH, had become a major source of income to poor rural households together with public transfers such as pensions and child allowances.[5]

7.3 RURAL CREDIT AND AGRICULTURAL EXTENSION TO SMALL FARMERS IN 1968

It is not possible to provide here a comprehensive assessment of all government programmes which bear directly or indirectly on the alleviation of rural poverty. Instead, the chapter concentrates on programmes of short-term credit and agricultural extension directed at small farmers, and draws on field work undertaken in 1968 and 1986 in nine communities located between Chiloé and Coquimbo.[6] The main focus is on the Institute of Agricultural Development (INDAP), which is one of the few government agencies to have maintained a continuous institutional presence in the countryside since the early 1960s.

INDAP's programmes

Until the coup of 1973, INDAP supplied credit through local Small Farmers' Committees. In 1968, when the initial survey was undertaken, over 2000 such committees had been formed with a total membership of 70 000 farmers. The largest number of committees was in the province of Cautín.

Loans were made under extremely favourable conditions to low income households.[7] The principal was not adjusted for inflation (running at around 30 per cent per annum in the 1960s), nominal interest rates were between 9 and 12 per cent per annum and no collateral, such as land with registered title, was required from borrowers. The only prerequisites were that (1) the borrower's main source of income should come from the farm for which the credit was requested; (2) the borrower should work this farm directly with his family and up to a maximum of three hired workers; (3) the borrower's net assets should not exceed a maximum of 25 times the minimum wage in the Department of Santiago in 1966: this gave a ceiling of US$19 500; and (4) the borrower must be a member of the local committee.[8]

Two types of credit were provided to small farmers. 'Community credits,' which amounted to 52 per cent of total INDAP credits in 1968, were one-year loans to purchase improved seed, fertiliser or simple materials to improve farm infrastructure, such as barbed wire or zinc sheets. 'Capitalisation credits', which amounted to 38 per cent of INDAP credits in 1968, were for much larger sums intended for the purchase of agricultural machinery or livestock. They were repayable over periods of up to five years, and were more selectively allocated to individuals with above-average management ability, who possessed the complementary resources required for success in the line of credit requested.[9] A third type of loan, called 'credits to peasant organisations' (usually co-operatives), amounted to only 10 per cent of total INDAP credit in 1968, and is not discussed further here.

In attempting an asssessment of INDAP's credit programme in the 1960s, two questions may be asked: (1) Did these loans reach the target group of poor farmers? and (2) What was the effect of these credits on farm productivity?

The first question can be answered with some precision at the national level. In their study of the distributive impact of public expenditure in Chile in 1969, Foxley *et al.* (1979) found that 50 per cent of the benefits associated with INDAP's programmes accrued to households with income levels of less than two minimum wages and 30 per cent of the benefits were received by households earning less than one minimum wage. No other programme in the agricultural sector, not even the land reform programme itself, delivered such a high proportion of its benefits to those in extreme poverty (Foxley *et al.*, 1979, p. 96).[10]

Assessing the productivity impact of INDAP credit and agricultural extension is more difficult. Research in progress may permit some conclusions to be drawn from the cross-section data of 1968 using multiple regression analysis. In the meantime, two simpler questions may be asked: (1) Did small farmers who received INDAP credits employ a superior agricultural technology to those who did not receive such credits? and (2) Were farmers with a high level of exposure to INDAP's extension

Table 7.3 Production credit and the use of chemical fertiliser and/or improved seed, 1968

	(Number of households)							
	No fert. or seed	Row (%)	Uses fert. or seed	Row (%)	Uses fert. and seed	Row (%)	Total	(%)
No credit	56	41	70	51	10	8	136	100
Col. (%)	74		61		29		61	
Uses credit	20	23	44	50	24	27	88	100
Col. (%)	26		39		71		39	
Total	76	34	114	51	34	15	224	100
Col. (%)	100		100		100		100	

$\chi^2 = 19.35$ DF = 2
Critical value of $\chi^2 = 5.99$ at 5 per cent significance level.

Source: ICIRA Small Farmers' Survey (1968).

activities more or less willing to turn to INDAP for advice if they had technical problems with their crops than farmers with low levels of such exposure?

An answer to the first question may be found in Tables 7.3 and 7.4 which contain information on the receipt of INDAP credit and the use of selected material inputs. Table 7.3 shows that 41 per cent of households without credit used neither chemical fertiliser nor improved seed in 1968, and only 8 per cent used both inputs. The corresponding figures for households with credit were 23 per cent and 27 per cent.

The positive association between credit and input use was confirmed by a χ^2 test. In Table 7.3, the value of χ^2 was more than twice the critical value at the 5 per cent level of significance.

The null hypothesis of there being no association between input use and receiving credit may therefore be rejected. The use of improved seed and chemical fertiliser in 1968 was significantly greater in those households receiving INDAP credits than in households not receiving such credit.

In Table 7.4, 80 per cent of households without credit used neither insecticide, herbicide nor fungicide, while 4 per cent used two or more of these inputs. The corresponding figures for households with credit were 65 per cent and 10 per cent. The value of χ^2 was marginally above the critical value at the 5 per cent level, so again the null hypothesis may be rejected.

Table 7.4   Production credit and the use of insecticide, herbicide and fungicide, 1968

| | (Number of households) | | | | | | | | | |
	Uses none	Row (%)	Uses one input	Row (%)	Uses two inputs	Row (%)	Uses three inputs	Row (%)	Total	(%)
No credit	109	80	22	16	4	3	1	1	136	100
Col. (%)	66		50		44		20		61	
Uses credit	57	65	22	25	5	6	4	4	88	100
Col. (%)	34		50		56		80		39	
Total	166	74	44	20	9	4	5	2	224	
Col. (%)	100		100		100		100		100	

$\chi^2 = 8.29$ DF = 3
Critical value of $\chi^2 = 7.81$ at 5 per cent significance level.

Source: ICIRA Small Farmers' Survey (1968).

However, in this case the rejection should be more cautious. While there appears to be a link between the use of insecticide, herbicide and fungicide (or some combination of these inputs) and the receipt of credit in 1868, this relationship is weaker than the connection between credit and the application of chemical fertiliser and/or improved seed.

Overall, these results suggest that in 1968 there was a significant statistical association between the receipt of INDAP credit and the level of agricultural technology employed by small farmers. However, the direction of causation between these two variables is less clear. Access to credit was not a necessary condition for small farmers to use a single element of an improved technology, such as fertiliser or improved seed, but adoption of a *combination* of improved inputs appears to have been much more difficult to achieve without credit. If peasants adopt innovations in an additive stepwise sequence, as suggested by Byerlee and Hesse de Polanco (1986), then the existence of credit rationing may inhibit diffusion. Such rationing certainly existed, as is made clear by the comments of many respondents who complained that they had not received as much credit as they had requested.

An answer to the second question above can be gleaned from Table 7.5 which shows the relationship between a household's

Table 7.5 Agricultural extension and identification of information sources for crop problem solving, 1968, number of households

Agricultural extension score (1)		Ask INDAP (2)	Row (%) (3)	Ask others (4)	Row (%) (5)	Total (6)	Row (%) (7)
0		0	0	78	100	78	100
	Col. (%)	0		48		41	
1		1	11	8	89	9	100
	Col. (%)	4		5		5	
2		0	0	8	100	8	100
	Col. (%)	0		5		4	
3		2	29	5	71	7	100
	Col. (%)	7		3		4	
4		1	14	6	86	7	100
	Col. (%)	4		4		4	
5		2	17	10	83	12	100
	Col. (%)	7		6		6	
6		0	0	8	100	8	100
	Col. (%)	0		5		4	
7		4	57	3	43	7	100
	Col. (%)	14		2		4	
8		3	43	4	57	7	100
	Col. (%)	11		2		4	
9		1	11	8	89	9	100
	Col. (%)	4		5		5	
10+		14	35	26	65	40	100
	Col. (%)	50		16		21	
Total		28	15	164	85	192	100
	Col. (%)	100		100		100	

$\chi^2 = 45.42$ DF $= 10$
Critical value of $\chi^2 = 18.3$ at 5 per cent significance level.

Notes: Column and row totals may not sum to 100 per cent due to rounding. Respondents who answered that they would not consult anyone if faced with a crop problem, are included in the 'Ask Others' category.

Source: ICIRA Small Farmers' Survey (1968).

exposure to agricultural extension from INDAP and its propensity to seek advice from INDAP to solve crop problems. Exposure to agricultural extension was measured by an index constructed from the answers to the following three questions included in the 1968 questionnaire:

(1) How many times in the last year were you visited on the farm by a member of INDAP's agricultural extension personnel?
(2) How many times in the last year were you called to a meeting of the local Small Farmers' Committee at which one of INDAP's agricultural extension personnel was present?
(3) How many times in the last year did you go to the local INDAP office to deal with issues concerning production credit or agricultural extension?

A visit from an agricultural extension officer to the farm was considered the most direct form of contact a small farmer could have, while a visit made to the local INDAP office was felt to be the least direct. In order to reflect this ranking, the following weighting system was employed. The answer to question (1) was multiplied by three, the answer to question (2) by two, and the answer to question (3) by one. The scores for each question were then summed to give the value of the household's agricultural extension index.

It should be pointed out that not all INDAP's field staff were trained agricultural extension officers in 1968. While some of them were agronomists or agricultural technicians (*técnicos agrícolas*), others were 'promoters' who had no technical qualifications in agriculture and were primarily concerned with organisational and administrative tasks, such as the establishment and supervision of Small Farmers' Committees. Since it is possible that contact with all types of INDAP personnel was included in the answers to the three questions above, the index may therefore have exaggerated in some cases the intensity of the problem-solving information flow from INDAP to small farmers.

The crop problem question was phrased as follows, 'If you have a problem with your crops, from whom would you seek advice?' It was an open question with a wide range of answers. Over half the respondents (57 per cent) declared that they would not seek advice from anyone, while 13 per cent stated they would turn to INDAP. The 'Others' category in Table 7.5 includes neighbours, relatives, unspecified agronomists and veterinary surgeons, and organisations located outside the community.

These data show that all of the 78 households who received no agricultural extension identified 'Others' as their source of crop problem-solving. Conversely, 35 per cent of farmers with a score of 7 or more on the agricultural extension index would have had recourse to INDAP.

Confirmation of a positive relationship between extension scores and a willingness to use INDAP was provided by two tests. The value of χ^2 in Table 7.5 was more than twice the critical value at the 5 per cent level of significance. The null hypothesis of there being no significant statistical association between exposure to agricultural extension and choosing INDAP to solve crop problems may therefore be rejected.

The expectation that the higher the level of exposure, the greater the propensity to turn to INDAP, was realised by regressing the number of households citing INDAP as a source of crop problem-solving (Table 7.5, column (2)) on the value of the agricultural extension index (Table 7.5 column (1)). The correlation coefficient was positive (R = + 0.62) and the regression coefficient on the extension index was positive and significant.[11]

However, there are problems in interpreting these results. In particular, the direction of causation is unclear. The reasoning given above assumes that it is the level of exposure which determines the degree of willingness to identify INDAP as an agent for solving crop problems. Nevertheless, it might be argued that causation runs in the opposite direction: households which view INDAP as a relevant source of technical advice are more likely to take advantage of its extension services.

Although this treats the perception of INDAP as exogenously given (e.g. by political criteria), there may be some truth in this view. In practice, causation is likely to run in both directions. After the formation of a local Small Farmers' Committee, a household becomes exposed to extension advice. If this advice proves useful, the household takes a positive view of INDAP and seeks further extension contacts.

What conclusions may be drawn from these data as to the effectiveness of INDAP's extension work in 1968? I believe that they provide support for such work. Whatever the direction of causation, the strong association between high levels of exposure to extension and a willingness to identify INDAP as a relevant agent for solving crop problems surely suggests that INDAP was meeting the needs of small farmers in one important area of productive activity.

In 1968–9, INDAP therefore performed well on both equity and efficiency criteria. It delivered a high proportion of its benefits to the lowest decile of the (rural) population and its subsidised credit programme led to the adoption of higher levels of agricultural technology among borrowers than among non-borrowers. Where exposure to its extension activities was high, INDAP was identified by small farmers as an important source of technical information for solving crop problems.

The evolution of INDAP's activities, 1968–86

Under the Popular Unity government (1970–3), INDAP's activities expanded significantly so that by September 1973 when Allende was overthrown by a military coup, there were more than 5000 staff on its payroll (Silva, 1990, p. 24). However, under the Pinochet administration (1973–90) which drastically reduced the size of the public sector, the INDAP's operations were sharply diminished. Between September 1973 and June 1980, INDAP's personnel was reduced by 74 per cent (Silva, 1990, p. 24).

This decline continued between 1980 and 1985, when the number of INDAP credit beneficiaries fell from 48 923 to 33 346; a reduction of 32 per cent (INDAP, 1986). Over the same period, the value of annual credit advanced by INDAP fell by more than half from US$38.5 million to US$18 million (INDAP, 1986).[12] The agency discontinued the direct provision of agricultural extension to small farmers and contracted out this task to private firms which have had a minimal impact (Silva, 1990, p. 28).

At the same time, INDAP developed a more diverse system of credits, each of which was targeted on a particular group of beneficiaries. By 1986, the agency offered five different types of credit compared to the three types supplied in 1968.[13] The most important type, which accounted for 86 per cent of INDAP credit supplied in 1985, was one-year credit for the purchase of seed, fertiliser and other intermediate inputs. This was similar to the community credit available in 1968 in that between 1983 and 1986, the nominal interest rate charged was 9 per cent while inflation was running at 24 per cent per annum, and no land titles were demanded as collateral. However, other terms of this type of credit were harder than in the 1960s. The principal was readjusted for inflation and a penalty interest rate (of 12.4 per cent) was levied on any unpaid principal for each day beyond 365 days.

A softer version of this type of credit was available in some years during the 1980s to the poorest farmers, who were identified by means testing.[14] These 'social support credits' had a maximum value of US$160 (in 1986) and could be used to purchase seed, fertiliser and barbed wire. They were repayable over one year at 6 per cent nominal interest without collateral, but the principal was adjusted for inflation.

Apart from a massive reduction in the scale of its credit operations and a general hardening of its loan conditions after 1973, INDAP changed its mode of operation from the mid-1970s. Instead of channelling credit to borrowers through local Small Farmers' Committees, INDAP transacted its business directly with each individual farmer and the Committees where abolished.

This was clearly a political move by the military government aimed at weakening popular organisations in the countryside. It will be argued below that the reconstitution of these committees is not only a prerequisite for giving small farmers a voice in the design and implementation of development policy, but it is also an organisational initiative which may bring important efficiency gains to the rural credit market.

Before attempting an evaluation of the changes in INDAP's policy after 1973, it is useful to review the incidence of INDAP credit between 1968 and 1986 among the households in the 1986 sample. Table 7.6 shows that nearly three-quarters of the sample (73 per cent) received credit from INDAP at some point during this period. Thus, in this sense, coverage by the agency of the small farmer population has been extensive.

However, half the sample either received no credit at all from INDAP between 1968 and 1986, or received it only up until 1974 when the Committees were dissolved. Only 14 per cent of households borrowed continuously from INDAP throughout the whole period, and nearly one-quarter (23 per cent) discontinued INDAP loans after the military coup. Indeed, the fact that 31 per cent of the sample received credit both before and after 1974 should not be interpreted as evidence of continuity. A considerable number of these households were supplied regularly with INDAP loans before 1974, but received credit for only one or two years after 1974.[15]

An assessment of neo-liberal credit policy

If the cross-section results from the 1968 data set are correct, then the declining expenditures by INDAP after 1973 are likely

Table 7.6   Number of households receiving INDAP credit, 1968–86

Community	Never	Period I only 1968–74	Period II only 1974–85	For part of both periods	Throughout both periods	Total
ICHUAC	2	2	1	6	7	18
Col. (%)	6	7	17	15	39	14
HUIFCO	5	7	2	5	0	19
Col. (%)	14	23	33	13	0	15
HUELEN	5	4	1	3	4	17
Col. (%)	14	13	17	8	22	13
HUAPI	5	5	0	6	1	17
Col. (%)	14	17	0	15	6	13
CARRIZALILLO	7	0	0	9	3	19
Col. (%)	20	0	0	22	17	15
LO ABARCA	2	0	2	2	3	9
Col. (%)	6	0	33	5	17	7
HUENTELAUQUEN	4	5	0	7	0	16
Col. (%)	11	17	0	18	0	12
LAS TAZAS	5	7	0	2	0	14
Col. (%)	14	23	0	5	0	11
Total	35 (27)	30 (23)	6 (5)	40 (31)	18 (14)	129
Col. (%)	100	100	100	100	100	100

Notes: Figures in parentheses are row percentages.
Column and row totals may not sum to 100 per cent due to rounding.

Source: Author's survey (1986).

to have had an adverse effect on the productivity and income
levels of small farmers. Indeed, the sharp rise in rural poverty
during the 1970s and early 1980s discussed earlier might now be
viewed as having been caused in part by the substantial contraction in INDAP's activities.

However, two arguments may be adduced in support of a
policy which reduces the long-run supply of credit from public
sources to finance working capital requirements in small farm
agriculture.

The graduation hypothesis

It might be argued that at an early stage of economic development when rural credit markets are unorganised, peasants have
little experience of contact with urban bureaucracies and great
potential exists for raising the productivity of small farm agriculture through a process of technical change embodied in in-

Table 7.7   Sources of production credit, 1968 and 1986

In 1968	No credit	Row (%)	INDAP credit	Row (%)	Other credit[a]	Row (%)	Total	(%)
			(Number of households) in 1986					
No credit	67	87	9	12	1	1	77	100
Col. (%)	57		41		20		53	
INDAP credit	42	78	9	17	3	5	54	100
Col. (%)	36		41		60		38	
Other credit	8	62	4	31	1	7	13	100
Col. (%)	7		18		20		9	
Total	117	81	22	15	5	4	144[b]	
Col. (%)	100		100		100		100	

Notes:

[a] Includes the State Bank, State Sugar Corporation, Institute for Indigenous Affairs (Temuco) and secondary borrowers from INDAP.

[b] A few households received credit from more than one credit source in 1968 or 1986. These households have more than one entry in Table 7.7.

Source: ICIRA Small Farmers' Survey (1968) and author's survey (1986).

termediate inputs (improved seed, fertiliser), there is a case for the state to supply this new technology temporarily through the channel of relatively indiscriminate subsidised credit.

However, as small farmers become more familiar with the administrative procedures of obtaining formal credit, as they accumulate knowledge of the new inputs and as their incomes grow, so they should be capable of switching from soft to hard sources of finance. They should 'graduate' from dependence on subsidised public funds to a reliance on credit from the commercial banks.

If this hypothesis were true in the present case, then as INDAP funds were cut back in the mid-1970s, so we should observe an increasing diversity of formal credit lines being used by small farmers. The information in Table 7.7 provides no support for this view. Of those households who received INDAP credit in 1968, 78 per cent obtained no production credit at all in 1986. Instead of graduating to become clients of the commercial banks, they had withdrawn from the formal capital market completely. In addition, 62 per cent of households who borrowed

from other formal sources in 1968, such as the State Bank and
the State Sugar Corporation (IANSA), had also withdrawn from
the formal credit market.

The increased liquidity hypothesis

Regardless of whether or not small farmers 'graduate' from soft
to hard sources of finance, it might be argued that a reduction in
the total volume of short-term credit to this sector, after a
deliberate 'supply-leading' phase in rural loans policy, would
not necessarily be harmful. Suppose that during an initial period
when credit for working capital was plentiful, farm productivity
and incomes rose. This would tend to be associated with an
increased capacity to save out of farm income and an incremental accumulation of farm assets.

Under these conditions, the liquidity constraint faced by small
farmers when funding their working capital requirements should
become less severe over time. Purchases of highly divisible intermediate inputs such as seed and fertiliser can be made either
out of the household's larger real balances or through seasonal
sales of assets, such as small livestock, which can be built up
again after the harvest. If this hypothesis were true, the link
between access to credit and the use of certain simple material
inputs would therefore become weaker over time owing to the
increased liquidity position of small farms.

This hypothesis can be tested with information from the 1986
sample shown in Tables 7.8 and 7.9. These data are presented in
a form which is directly comparable to the figures shown in
Tables 7.3 and 7.4 which are based on the 1968 sample. Before
discussing the results, two caveats should be mentioned.

First, households were divided into recipients and non-recipi-
ents of credit on the basis of whether they had taken out loans for
the agricultural year 1985–6. There were several cases of farmers
using fertiliser in 1985–6 which they had obtained with credit
received in a previous year. This will tend to bias the results in
favour of the 'increased liquidity' hypothesis.

Secondly, the use of a given set of material inputs as indicators
of the level of agricultural technology employed, suggests that
farm-level production functions are invariant across the different
farm systems encountered in the nine communities. This is not
strictly true. In particular, chemical fertilisers are not used for

cereals on rain-fed land in Huentelauquén and Las Tazas for fear of burning the crop roots in dry years.

Despite these qualifications, the information contained in Tables 7.3, 7.4, 7.8 and 7.9 offers an interesting opportunity for analysing the stability of any observed relationships between agricultural credit and material input use over time in a wide variety of traditional small farming communities.

Table 7.8 shows that 62 per cent of households without credit used either improved seed or fertiliser or both, while the corresponding figure for those with credit was 100 per cent. This suggests that there was still a positive association between the receipt of credit and material input use in 1986.

The value of χ^2 in Table 7.8 was more than twice the critical value at the 5 per cent level of significance, so the null hypothesis was rejected. Although the direction of causation cannot be established with certainty, these results suggest that access to formal credit may continue to be a significant factor explaining the use of chemical fertiliser and/or improved seed in 1986. The value of χ^2 for Table 7.8 was only slightly smaller than for Table 7.3, which is based on data from 1968.

The most striking difference between Tables 7.3 and 7.8 concerns input use by those households with credit. Whereas in 1968 27 per cent of those with credit used both fertiliser and improved seed, and 23 per cent used neither input, the corresponding figures in 1986 were 8 per cent and 0 per cent. Borrowers who in 1968 took out loans for home improvements, such as zinc sheets, had been squeezed out of the capital market altogether, while those who did borrow to cover working capital needs were more parsimonious in their use of modern inputs.

Table 7.9 shows that only 21 per cent of households without credit used insecticide and/or herbicide and/or fungicide in 1986. The corresponding figure for households with credit was 40 per cent. In this case, the value of χ^2 was marginally below the critical value at the 5 per cent level, so the null hypothesis cannot be rejected.

This suggests that the use of insecticide, herbicide and fungicide was not associated with the receipt of formal credit in 1986. In fact, the relative frequencies in the cells of Table 7.9 are very similar to those in Table 7.4. However, less than one-quarter (24 per cent) of the 1986 sample used one or more of these inputs, and where usage did occur, it was in very small quantities.

Table 7.8 Production credit and the use of chemical fertiliser and/or improved seed, 1986

	(Number of households)							
	No fert. or seed	Row (%)	Uses fert. or seed	Row (%)	Uses fert. and seed	Row (%)	Total	(%)
No credit	42	38	61	55	7	7	110	100
Col. (%)	100		73		78		81	
Uses credit	0	0	23	92	2	8	25	100
Col. (%)	0		27		22		19	
Total	42	31	84	62	9	7	135	100
Col. (%)	100		100		100		100	

$\chi^2 = 14.00$ DF = 2
Critical value of $\chi^2 = 5.99$ at 5 per cent significance level.

Source: Author's survey (1986).

Table 7.9 Production credit and the use of insecticide, herbicide and fungicide, 1986

	(Number of households)						
	Uses none	Row (%)	Uses one input	Row (%)	Uses two inputs	Row (%)	Total	(%)
No credit	89	79	19	17	4	4	112	100
Col. (%)	86		73		57		82	
Uses credit	15	60	7	28	3	12	25	100
Col. (%)	14		27		43		18	
Total	104	76	26	19	7	5	137	
Col. (%)	100		100		100		100	

$\chi^2 = 5.17$ DF = 2
Critical value of $\chi^2 = 5.99$ at 5 per cent significance level.

Source: Author's survey (1986).

Overall, these results are not consistent with the predictions of the 'increased liquidity' hypothesis. Short-term credit possibly remains an important channel through which small farmers may gain access to improved agricultural technology and, thereby, increase agricultural productivity and farm incomes.

7.4 RURAL DEVELOPMENT STRATEGIES FOR TRADITIONAL SMALLHOLDING COMMUNITIES DURING THE 1990s

However, it is clear that in many poor rural communities the marginal social return to investment in agriculture is low. This is most likely in areas of low rainfall and/or where the physical resource base is weak and deteriorating further through soil erosion and declining soil fertility.

It is therefore essential that government policy during the 1990s moves beyond the narrow aim of promoting agricultural growth to a much wider concern with fostering rural development. The final section of the chapter examines the implications of such a policy shift for the design of rural credit programmes. In particular, an attempt is made to define appropriate roles for the major actors in the current institutional framework.

Farm-oriented and household-oriented programmes

In an article on investment strategies to alleviate rural poverty in Latin America, de Janvry and Sadoulet (1989) distinguish between Farm-oriented (FOPs) and Household-oriented (HOPs) programmes. Farm-oriented programmes are targeted at peasant farmers who have access to sufficient land to derive most of their income from own-crop and livestock production. Such enterprises have some potential for agricultural growth in the medium and long run. The objective of FOPs is to raise agricultural productivity and farm incomes.

Household-oriented programmes are aimed at the poorest farmers with very little land who generate most of their income through off-farm employment. The aim of such programmes is to increase incomes through self-employment at the household or community level in activities outside commercial agriculture, or to reduce real expenditures by the household in meeting basic needs.

Hitherto, INDAP has been exclusively concerned with Farm-oriented programmes. These are important and have a central place in any rural development strategy but they need to be complemented with HOPs, which INDAP, as of 1986, was ill-equipped to supply. Such Household-oriented programmes as have been introduced were initiatives taken by other government agencies, such as the Gold Plan administered by the State Mining Corporation (ENAMI), the Grant Scheme for Self-help Rural Housing run by the Ministry of Housing, and the many local projects sponsored by non-governmental organisations such as the *Grupo de Investigaciones Agrarias*. The experience of other countries such as Mexico and Bolivia suggests that a wide variety of HOPs might be feasible, particularly in agro-industry, handicrafts and tourism.

Creation of local committees of rural development

At present, if party political organisations are excluded, there are four major actors in rural development; individual households, central government agencies (such as INDAP), local government; and NGOs (including Church organisations). To this group there needs to be added a fifth element – local Committees of Rural Development (CRDs). These would not simply be a reincarnation of the Small Farmers' Committees established by the previous Christian Democrat administration in the 1960s. They would be concerned not just with agriculture but would take an integrated multisectoral approach capable of embracing both Farm-oriented and Household-oriented programmes.

In consequence, it will be necessary for the activities of CRDs to be co-ordinated by municipal or commune-level boards. These boards would have a majority of elected representatives from the CRDs and an *ex officio* membership drawn from the municipal council (the mayor as chairman?), local representatives of relevant public sector institutions such as INDAP and non-governmental organisations. If these boards were to manage resources channelled from the government's Social Investment Fund (FOSIS), they would need to draw on technical expertise in accounting and finance.

The local CRDs would play a dual role. On the one hand, they would promote popular participation in the rural development process and articulate local initiatives and demands. This will meet the criticism that, although the military government's welfare programmes were effectively targeted, they were too narrowly defined and implemented in an authoritarian manner – e.g. the emergency employment programmes (PEM and POJH) (Graham, 1990, p. 7). On the other hand, it can be argued that the creation of a network of CRDs might enhance the efficiency of the rural credit market and improve the delivery system for rural (including agricultural) extension and training.

Taking the extension issue first, it should be noted that whatever rural development strategy is implemented during the 1990s it should ensure institutional flexibility at the local level. This means that in areas where NGOs have worked successfully with local communities for several years, and may have ongoing projects, the relevant CRDs may choose to receive agricultural extension advice from the NGOs which would be paid by the municipal board with resources from FOSIS. In other areas, where no such NGO presence exists, it may be necessary for INDAP to resume its previous extension role. Which of these institutional alternatives is selected should be decided at a regional and/or local level.

Otherwise, the extension and training argument for establishing CRDs is that much relevant information is not farm or household-specific, and that disseminating such information enjoys scale economies over a wide range of output. It costs no more for an agronomist to travel to a rural community and speak to an audience of 30 persons at a meeting of the CRD than it does for him to address an audience of two.

The capital market case for the establishment of CRDs is by no means clear cut. In 1986, INDAP supplied short-term loans to rural households without any intermediation. The requirement of a guarantor for each loan ensured an element of peer group monitoring (Stiglitz, 1990) and in case of default, both borrowers and guarantor were denied further credit until the debt was repaid. In return for sharing the borrower's risk, many guarantors obtained INDAP credit for themselves through the borrower increasing his loan request to include a component which was assigned to the guarantor. For this reason, it is necessary to distinguish between formal (or primary) and informal (or secondary) borrowers from INDAP.

The most plausible efficiency argument requires that some rural credit should be supplied not to individual households, or even pairs of households, but to self-selected groups of up to five or six households which could come together under the aegis of the CRD. Under this arrangement, the group would be collectively responsible for the debts of each of its members. If such a scheme, modelled on the experience of the Grameen Bank in Bangladesh, were to operate successfully, then it could reduce transactions costs in the credit market (1) by reducing the number of loans for a given volume of credit supplied by the lender, and (2) by reducing the amount of time spent by borrowers on loan-related administrative tasks. By spreading risks more widely among borrowers, it might also increase the repayment rate.

Finally, the establishment of CRDs might facilitate the identification of new socially profitable projects through encouraging group discussion, and this would improve capital market efficiency. Once they are operating effectively to provide rural credit, extension and training, these committees could develop in several directions, including trial schemes of crop insurance.

Rural development as adaptive sequencing

The strong interdependence which exists between different programmes such as credit and extension, or health and education, provides the central rationale for adopting a strategy of 'integrated rural development' (IRD) (de Janvry, 1981, pp. 224–54). This approach which has continued to evolve since its introduction in the late 1960s, has led to the design of complex multisectoral programmes requiring close co-ordination of activities by public sector institutions.

However, IRD projects make heavy demands on a very scarce input, namely competent public sector administrative capacity at the regional and local level. For this reason, it is preferable to define priorities more narrowly and identify sequences of activity which involve different policy agents (both public and private) at different points in time. This strategy of 'adaptive sequencing' embodies a disequilibrium dynamic very similar to that of unbalanced growth (Hirschman, 1958; Johnston and Clark, 1982, pp. 225–7).

The example of a small-scale tourist project in one of the communities may illustrate what this approach means in practice. The market for domestic tourism, recreation and leisure services in Latin American countries is segmented. High income groups will demand facilities comparable to those provided to North American or West European visitors, but middle and low income groups whose aggregate purchasing power may be considerable, are much less exigent. It is to the latter groups that impoverished rural communities which enjoy the benefits of a good location for supplying simple recreational facilities must appeal.

The community concerned is intersected by the Panamerican Highway and possesses several miles of Pacific coastline. At one point, the road comes close to a small beach, where it was noted that cars would sometimes stop during the holiday season for an hour or two to break a long journey. One year, the community authorities installed drinking water at the beach and this was enough to induce several travellers to spend a night there in a tent or caravan.

The next year, toilets and showers were built. This prompted some families to spend several days at the site. The following year a small shop was set up to serve the visitors and a dynamic sequence had begun. By 1986, the next step, which required local government approval, was to have been the installation of a bar and restaurant followed by the construction of several beach cabins.

Other opportunities for this type of locally-controlled tourist development exist in Chile. It offers one of the most promising avenues for non-agricultural rural growth for communities with a poor agricultural resource base, but good road access.

Adaptive sequencing also provides a framework for introducing Farm-oriented programmes which will allow participating institutions to specialise in those activities where they enjoy a comparative advantage. NGOs excel at generating new ideas and introducing policy innovations at local level, because they enjoy close working relationships with the intended beneficiaries and they recruit young, energetic and highly motivated staff who work in an organisational environment which encourages personal initiative and minimises bureaucratic procedure. However, their lack of resources prevents any generalised diffusion of their 'successes' and inhibits the development of 'linkages' from one project to another.

In the institutional context outlined above, NGOs could discuss a new idea with the municipal board and/or local CRD in an area, and then launch a pilot programme with the participation of a few families. If the initiative proved successful, it could be further refined and diffused locally through the CRDs. In exceptional cases, such an initiative could be incorporated into the regional activities of a government agency such as INDAP.

7.5   CONCLUSION

Although absolute poverty is not as widespread in Chile as in many other Latin American countries, the extent of deprivation in 1990 is likely to have been at least as great, if not greater, than twenty years earlier. The headcount ratio rose sharply between 1970 and the early 1980s, and more than doubled in the rural areas. Since 1983, the labour market has tightened, but by 1989 the unemployment rate was still significantly above the 1970 level, while real wages were little more than when Allende took office (*World Development Report*, 1990, p. 119). For this reason, poverty alleviation is a major priority of the Aylwin administration.

In the light of current debates over anti-poverty programmes in Chile, it may be useful to assess the experience of the rural credit and agricultural extension schemes directed by INDAP at small farmers since the mid-1960s. This target group includes some of the poorest households in the country, while the existence of a panel data set for 1968 and 1986 permits the testing of several hypotheses.

The results of the analysis suggest that in 1968–9, INDAP performed well in terms of both equity and efficiency. In contrast to many subsidised credit schemes in other developing countries, the INDAP programme delivered a high proportion of its benefits to the lowest decile of the (rural) population. The programme may have also prompted the use of higher levels of agricultural technology among borrowers than among non-borrowers. Where exposure to its extension activities was high, INDAP was identified by small farmers as an important source of technical information for solving crop problems.

The massive contraction in INDAP's activities after 1973 must have contributed to the increased incidence of rural poverty observed in the 1980s. In 1968, 53 per cent of the ICIRA sample of small farmers did not receive production credit and 59 per cent received no agricultural extension. In 1986, these figures had risen to 81 per cent and 92 per cent respectively.

Life-cycle factors may partly explain these changes. The 1986 sample contained a high proportion of elderly household heads, some of whom received pensions and worked less intensively in agriculture than in 1968. However, household heads who were inactive in agriculture have been excluded from these calculations, and many households with a pensioner contained at least one young adult who worked the family holding.

The net effect on rural welfare of replacing support schemes for small farmers as producers by emergency employment programmes is difficult to calculate. It is necessary to deduct from the value of gross earnings under the PEM or POJH an amount which corresponds to the decline in farm output as a result of (1) lower crop yields following the reduced use of intermediate inputs (particularly, improved seed and chemical fertiliser), and (2) any reduction in the cultivated area.

Strategies of poverty alleviation among small farmers during the 1990s should move beyond a narrow concentration on agricultural growth embodied in Farm-oriented programmes to a much wider concept of rural development incorporating Household-oriented projects. This shift in policy emphasis requires complementary institutional reforms. In particular, local CRDs need to be (re-)established and integrated into a broader framework within which local authorities and non-governmental organisations must play a more important role than in the past. Only in this way will the objectives of FOSIS be achieved.

Notes

1. The author wishes to thank David Hojman for his comments on an earlier draft of this paper and the Grupo de Investigaciones Agrarias for their collaboration in the 1986 survey which was funded by a grant from the Economic and Social Research Council (ESRC). Financial assistance from the following organisations to analyse the 1986 data is gratefully acknowledged: London School of Economics Staff Research Fund; Suntory/Toyota International Centre for Economics and Related Disciplines (ST/ICERD); and the Leverhulme Trust.

2. Note that the sale of pigs was a traditional way of smoothing household consumption over the year and raising livestock was one of the few channels for accumulating tangible assets open to low income rural households.

3. See Pablo Neruda's account of hunting wild swans in the Lake in his *Memoirs* (1978, p. 18).

4. During the 1980s in Chiloé, there was a boom in the extraction of a particular seaweed (*gracilaria*, commonly known as *pelillo*) for sale to Japan. This led to the temporary migration of many poor families from the mainland who set up camp along the shore of the gulf of Quetalmahue near Ancud.

5. The process of land redistribution which has transformed the agrarian structure since the mid-1960s has not increased the holdings of traditional small farmers. The reason for this is that the criteria used for defining agrarian reform beneficiaries under the Frei (1964–70) and Allende (1970–3) administrations gave priority to the permanent workers on the expropriated estates. Thus, none of the household heads in our 1968 sample qualified as permanent individual beneficiaries of the land reform. Only two of their descendants were assigned plots which they still owned in 1986 (Scott, 1990, p. 74).

   In retrospect, the significance of agrarian reform in Chile has been to reduce the landed wealth and political power of the largest land owners. Land reform has not proved in the long run an effective instrument for the elimination of rural poverty. Consequently, it is unlikely that calls for further compulsory redistributions of land will feature on the political agenda during the 1990s.

6. For further details on these communities, see Scott (1990).

7. The recovery rate for INDAP credit (75 per cent) was higher than for loans advanced to land reform beneficiaries by CORA (48 per cent), while the subsidy component was lower (i.e. 51 per cent as compared to 63 per cent) (Foxley *et al.*, 1979, p. 92).

8. By comparison, the State Bank which was another public sector institution providing agricultural credit required from its borrowers; (1) the land title to the borrowers' holding; (2) a guarantor who was also a farmer and had a bank account; and (3) an inventory of the borrower's assets. The first two conditions alone would have excluded the majority of INDAP credit beneficiaries.

   For further details on lending by INDAP and the State Bank during the 1960s, see Nisbet (1967).

9. The asset ceiling for capitalisation credits was raised to US$ 27 250.

10. The corresponding figures for land reform expenditures were 62 per cent and 20 per cent respectively.

11. For completeness, the number of households citing other sources for crop problem-solving (Table 7.5, column 3,) was regressed on the agricultural extension index (Table 7.5, column 1). As expected, the correlation coefficient was negative, but the regression coefficient on the extension index was negative and insignificant at the 5 per cent level.

12. This underestimates the true decline since these figures are given in nominal US dollars.

13. The five types of credit were: (1) short-term individual credit (for seed and fertiliser); (2) long-term individual credit (construction materials, livestock); (3) credit for land clearance; (4) social support credit; and (5) resettlement credit (for certain ex-members of privatised producer cooperatives who did not wish to accept land parcels after decollectivisation).

   In 1986, the eligibility criteria for INDAP loans were (1) to farm a holding of less than 12 basic irrigated hectares (b.i.h.); (2) to possess net assets of less than 3500 UF (US$56 000); and (3) to derive not less than 60 per cent of earnings from agriculture.

14. All credit applicants to INDAP had to complete a schedule which, *inter alia*, contained an estimate of current income.

15. Some of these households were excluded by INDAP as a result of having incurred debts with the agency.

References

Byerlee, D. and Hesse de Polanco, E. (1986) 'Farmers' Stepwise Adoption of Technological Packages: Evidence from the Mexican Altiplano', *American Journal of Agricultural Economics* (August).

De Janvry, A. (1981) *The Agrarian Question and Reformism in Latin America* (Baltimore: Johns Hopkins University Press).

De Janvry, A., Sadoulet, E. and Wilcox, L. (1986) *Rural Labour in Latin America*, WEP Research Working Paper (Geneva: International Labour Office).

De Janvry, A. and Sadoulet, E. (1989) 'Investment Strategies to Combat Rural Poverty: A Proposal for Latin America', *World Development*, vol. 17, no. 8 (August).

De Los Reyes, P. (1990) 'The Rural Poor: Survival Strategies and Living Conditions among the Rural Population in the Seventh Region', in D. E. Hojman (ed.), *Neo-liberal Agriculture in Rural Chile* (London: Macmillan).

Derksen, M. M. J. (1990) 'Santa Sabina: Surviving in a Rural Shanty Town', in D. E. Hojman (ed.), *Neo-Liberal Agriculture in Rural Chile* (London: Macmillan).

ECLAC (1985) 'La Pobreza en América Latina: Dimensiones y Políticas', *Estudios e Informes de la ECLAC*, no. 54 (Santiago).

Foxley, A. *et al.* (1979) *Redistributive Effects of Government Programmes: The Chilean Case* (Oxford: Pergamon Press).

Gómez, S. (1987) 'Estrategia de Sobrevivencia en el medio rural; los trabajadores temporeros', in Urzúa, R. and Dooner, P. (eds), *La Opción Preferencial por los Pobres: de la teoría a la práctica* (Santiago: CISOC–Bellarmino).

Graham, C. (1990) 'From Emergency Employment to Social Investment: Changing Approaches to Poverty Alleviation in Chile', paper presented to CERC–ILAS–St Anthony's College Conference on the Transition to Democracy in Chile.

Hirschman, A. O. (1958) *The Strategy of Economic Development* (New Haven: Yale University Press).

INDAP (1986) Data provided to author by Sr Joaquín de la Fuente, Head of Operations, Santiago.

Jarvis, L. S. (1985) *Chilean Agriculture under Military Rule: From Reform to Reaction, 1973–1980*, Research Series, no. 59 (Berkeley: Institute of International Studies, University of California).

Johnston, B. F. and Clark, W. C. (1982) *Redesigning Rural Development: A Strategic Perspective* (Baltimore: Johns Hopkins University Press).

Neruda, P. (1978) *Memoirs* (London: Penguin).

Nisbet, C. T. (1967) 'Supervised Credit Programs for Small Farmers in Chile', *Inter-American Economic Affairs*, vol. 21, no. 2 (Autumn).

ODEPLAN-IEUC (1975; 1986) *Mapa de la Extrema Pobreza* (Santiago).

ODEPLAN (1984) *Informe Social 1983* (Santiago).

Ortega, E. and Tironi, E. (1988) *Pobreza en Chile* (Santiago: Centro de Estudios del Desarrollo).

Pollack, M. and Uthoff, A. (1986) *El Mercado de Trabajo y la Pobreza en Chile, 1969–1984* (Santiago) (mimeo).

Raczynski, D. (1986) ¿Disminuyó la pobreza entre 1970 y 1982?, *Notas Técnicas*, no. 90 (Santiago: CIEPLAN).

Ramírez, P. (1968) *Cambio en las formas de pago a la mano de obra agrícola* (Santiago: ICIRA).

Rivera, R. and Cruz, M. E. (1984) *Pobladores Rurales. Cambios en el Poblamiento y el Empleo Rural en Chile* (Santiago: Grupo de Investigaciones Agrarias).

Rodríguez, J. (1985) *La Distribución del Ingreso y El Gasto Social en Chile – 1983* (Santiago: ILADES).

Scott, C. D. (1990) 'Land Reform and Poverty Rights among Small Farmers in Chile, 1968–86', in D. E. Hojman (ed.), *Neo-liberal Agriculture in Rural Chile* (London: Macmillan).

Silva, P. (1990) 'State Subsidiarity in the Chilean Countryside', in D. E. Hojman (ed.), *Neo-liberal Agriculture in Rural Chile* (London: Macmillan).

Stiglitz, J. E. (1990) 'Peer Monitoring and Credit Markets', *World Bank Economic Review*, vol. 4, no. 3 (September).

Torche, A. (1987) 'Distribuir el ingreso para satisfacer las necesidades básicas', in F. Larraín (ed.), *Desarrollo económico en democracia* (Santiago: Universidad Católica).

Urzúa, R. (1984) 'Caracterización, dimensiones y evolución de la pobreza rural', in *Estudios sobre la Pobreza Rural* (Rome: United Nations Food and Agriculture Organisation).

Valdés, A. (1971) 'Wages and Schooling of Agricultural Workers in Chile', *Economic Development and Cultural Change* (January).

Valdés, X. (1988) 'Feminización del Mercado de Trabajo Agrícola: Las Temporeras', in *Mundo de Mujer: Continuidad y Cambio* (Santiago: Centro de Estudios de la Mujer).

Vergara, C. (1987) Book review, ¿Disminuyó la pobreza?, in *Proposiciones*, no. 13, SUR (Santiago).

World Bank (1990) *World Development Report 1990* (Washington, D.C.: World Bank).

8 Agricultural Policies, Technological Gap, and Peasant Farming: From Pinochet to Aylwin
Guy Durand

The time has come for an assessment of the situation after the return of democracy to Chile following 17 years of military dictatorship. Although the first period of the Pinochet regime was a painful one from a political, social and economic point of view, including two deep recessions (in 1975–6 and 1982–3), after 1983 the economy took an upward trend: a 5.4 per cent annual growth of Gross National Product (GNP) between 1984 and 1989, the unemployment rate falling from 18.7 per cent in 1983 to 6.5 per cent in 1989, the doubling of exports, and a decrease in foreign debt after 1985 (Díaz, 1989).

Agricultural production increased slowly. After the crisis of 1982–3, the balance of agricultural trade continued to improve, reaching $1300 million in 1988–9 (*Revista del Campo*, 12 March 1990). There is no denying, however, that the growth of the agricultural sector has entailed contradictory developments: a regular, and indeed ever-increasing growth in exports of fruit and timber, but at the same time a considerable fall in the production of staple foods until 1982 (cereals, sugar, oil-producing plants). The latter suffered from foreign competition following the general opening up of the national frontiers. In spite of the pressure brought to bear on the price of food, and the restriction of *per capita* consumption, the cost in foreign currency of food imports threatened the macroeconomic balance. A change in policy was thought to be necessary, involving a progressive return to protectionist measures and new price guarantees for producers.

By the end of the 1980s, a practically complete food import substitution had come into effect. The Aylwin government, coming to office in March 1990, realised the importance of agriculture for

149

economic development, but also saw how frail the results were. How was agriculture going to develop? The problems were:

(1) First, the significant running into debt of farmers who had invested more than 2300 million dollars in the process of modernisation, more than half of this amount being considered as bad debt,

(2) Secondly, the fragility of export markets concentrated on specific products (apples, grapes), and specific countries (in particular the USA).

(3) Finally, the proposed reforms of agricultural taxation and of the legislation of seasonal labour, considered as threats by commercial farmers.

The plight of seasonal labourers, whose number went up from 30 per cent of the total of agricultural workers in 1964 to nearly 70 per cent in 1990, and that of peasant farmers marginalised by the process of capitalist modernisation, was bleak.

The '*Concertación Democrática*' (democratic coalition) which brought Aylwin to power asserted its willingness to pay off the 'social debt' owed to the peasant farmers. The avowed target was to do all that was possible to bring them back into the national economy, within the framework of a policy advocating rural development, which would bring to the fore the productive potential of peasant farming neglected by the previous regime.

In the following sections, the specific traits of this peasant farming are described, together with the type of marginalisation it has undergone. Special attention is given to the way in which the technological gap between peasant farms, and medium-sized and big farm holdings has widened and been strengthened by the technological transfer policy implemented since 1982. We then address the question of to what extent new policies, enforced since March 1990, are permitting the reintegration of peasant farming.

8.1 PEASANT FARMING: THE HIDDEN FACE OF MODERNISATION

The aim of the military junta had been for productive resources to be allocated once more by the market. The state was no longer to intervene in the economy, and trade union power was to be destroyed. In the agrarian sector, the state would withdraw the technical and financial assistance previously granted to farmers. Development, therefore, was one-sided: medium and large-scale farming of a capitalist type was emerging, which employed more and more seasonal labour for the production of fruit for export, whereas many peasant farmers were reduced to poverty. Nevertheless, peasant farming did not disappear from the scene but it either put up defensive structures (Vio Grossi, 1990) or fell into what has been known as '*campesinización pauperizante*' (Rivera, 1988).

The new traits of peasant farming

Peasant farming in the 1980s was shaped by different factors: first, the traditional *minifundio* resulting from crop sharing throughout generations since the colonial period, then the land ceded to the Mapuche Indians at the end of the nineteenth century, the small farms allocated in the course of several programmes of colonisation since the beginning of the twentieth century, and finally the plots of land resulting from the agrarian counter-reform (Echeñique, 1989). Most authors agree about the specific traits of this peasant farming: labour drawn mainly from the family, limited availability of capital and technology, and dependence on the market. However, Chilean peasant farming is not as homogeneous as it might seem. Various factors intervene to explain the differences in prosperity: land surface, water resources, access and means of communication, agro-ecological and geographical situation, profile of the family unit (Vio Grossi, 1990).

Contrary to many South-American countries, peasant farming in Chile is not all to be found in marginal zones, as more than 40 per cent of the peasant land is in the Central Valley, and 25 per cent is irrigated. This comparatively favourable geographical position, resulting from the land reforms, was not enough to prevent the process of marginalisation in the 1970s and 1980s.

The number of smallholdings would be about 210 000 (300 000 people representing 37.5 per cent of the active agricultural population) according to Echeñique and Rolando's (1989) calculations based on the employment survey of the National Statistics Institute, and defining as peasants the independent, agricultural workers and unpaid members of their families. Ortega's estimate is 250 000, based on data on arable land, economically active agricultural population and number of active members per family. This leads Ortega to the definition of a peasant farm as that under 6.3 h.r.b.[1] (Vio Grossi, 1990)

Marginalisation and technological gap

The share of peasant farming in production has not ceased to decline, especially during the 1980s. Marginalisation took on the character of a progressive eviction from production to the benefit of the medium-sized and big estates, owing, specifically, to the widening of the gap in farming productivity. This has led some authors to speak of the technological gap (Echeñique, 1989).

According to Rojas (quoted by Echeñique, 1989), in 1980, out of the total land used for each of these crops, peasant farmers grew 57 per cent of annual crops (cereals), 71 per cent of vegetables (greens and orchard output) and 50 per cent of fruit and vines. In 1987, the estimations of Echeñique based on value participation resulted in only 28 per cent for annual crops, 53 per cent for vegetables and 16 per cent for fruit and vines.

Whereas, according to the admitted standards of rural economics, gross production and added value per hectare tend to decrease as the farming area increases (Berry and Cline, 1979), the situation is reversed in Chile. Table 8.1 presents a comparison of average yields per crop between smallholding and medium-sized and big farm holdings.

These gaps are disturbing and may give rise to some hypotheses concerning the process of marginalisation. Indeed, a globally favourable price policy after the 1982–3 crisis, together with a certain stabilisation of land distribution (agrarian reform and counter-reform) were favourable factors for the revival of a sort of 'green revolution', taking place at the same time as a strong expansion in the fruit sector. The differential impact of this 'green revolution' on productivity was all the more important as official support for peasant farming had practically disappeared. The widest gaps concern the crops for which there has been the most important technical development during this period. On the other hand, productions which have benefited from financial and technical support by agri-business industries have suffered less from the technological gap. This is the case of sugarbeet,

Table 8.1   Yields in peasant farms, and medium-sized and big farm holdings (100 kg/ha), 1986–7

Crops	Peasant farms	Medium-sized and big estates	Gap (%)
WIDE GAPS			
Dry wheat (South)	22.2	35.6	−60.4
Dry oats	15.1	26.7	−77.1
Irrigated corn	62.0	86.5	−39.5
Beans for home market	9.4	12.4	−31.5
Dry sunflower seeds	14.1	34.0	−140.9
Potatoes	96.0	158.9	−65.5
NARROW GAPS			
Irrigated rice	38.3	40.3	−5.1
Lentils (South)	5.2	5.6	−8.4
Chick peas	8.4	10.6	−25.6
NO GAP OR POSITIVE GAP			
Irrigated beet	516.6	518.2	−0.3
Rape	21.9	20.4	+6.8
Tobacco	29.5	30.7	−4.1
Export beans	11.7	12.9	−10.6
Dry barley (South)	35.4	27.1	+23.6

Note: Small differences may appear because of rounding.

Source: Echeñique and Rolando (1989) p. 60.

rape, export beans and tobacco. For these crops the main difficulty has often been access to production contracts. The yield gap does not seem significant in the case of rice, lentils and chickpeas, for which there have only been small technological changes during the 1980s.

8.2   SUPPORT FOR PEASANT FARMING: FROM PINOCHET TO AYLWIN

Failure of a liberal policy

The experts of the Pinochet administration attributed the low productivity of the efforts made in favour of agriculture during the period preceding 1973 to the difficulty of transferring land expropriated by agrarian reform to the private sector, and to strong intervention by the state (Hurtado *et al.*, 1990). Agriculture was also suffering from discriminatory measures: nil or negative protection, and comparatively low prices (urban bias) sometimes compensated for by subsidies to imports and credit.

The expression of the comparative advantages pertaining to agriculture was to benefit from the policies of liberalisation of prices and of realistic exchange rates, and from the dismantling of protectionist systems concerning products and factors. Although a start was made in export-oriented production (specifically apples and table grapes), basic food production fell, as has already been said.[2] At the beginning of the 1980s, during the worst phase of the recession, 48 per cent of the calories and 30 per cent of the proteins consumed by Chileans came from imported food. The share of imports in home consumption reached 66 per cent for wheat, 97 per cent for vegetable oils and 50 per cent for sugar (Gómez and Echeñique, 1988).

Faced with failure of the liberal measures, the Minister of Agriculture Jorge Prado gave a new twist to his agricultural policy: a mild protectionism was re-established, together with some public purchase monopolies and price guarantees. At the same time a technology transfer policy was set up. Is it possible to gauge to what extent this policy contributed to the gap between industrial farming and peasant farming?

Technology transfer programmes

The evolution of the technology transfer programmes implemented throughout the 1980s reveals the changing attitude of the Pinochet administration toward the agricultural sector. Efforts were concentrated on the modernisation of farms through the adoption of new technology, transferred, after a research period, to those farmers who were the most able to receive it: industrial farmers and 'economically viable' farmers. The peasant farmers merely benefited from social measures.

From the industrial farmer . . . (technology transfer groups) . . .

As early as 1982, a first programme was proposed, to put at the disposal of industrial farmers some tested technology likely to increase productivity. The INIA (National Institute of Agronomical Research) was responsible for its implementation by appointing one research-developer for a group of 20 farmers in a homogeneous agro-ecological zone. This constituted by definition a GTT (Technology Transfer Group). These industrial farmers were selected according to their land surface, which had to be over 12 h.r.b. They represented roughly 35 000 farms throughout the country, controlling more than 50 per cent of the agricultural land. By 1988, INIA had managed to organise 132 GTTs grouping 1980 farmers with an average of 490 physical hectares per farm. The INIA personnel were at their disposal for four years, after which the GTTs were supposed to take part in the financing of technological support. This second emancipatory stage was reached by 68 groups in 1987–8 (Larraín, 1989).

To the 'economically viable' farmer (Total Technology Transfer programmes)

Another programme called the PTTI (Total Technology Transfer programme) came into being in 1983 under the responsibility of INDAP (Institute of Agricultural Development). Its originality lies in two directions: its target population and the means of implementation. Its declared aim was to integrate into the national economy the small and medium-sized farms whose land surface was fewer than 12 h.r.b. by means of technical support, credit, management guidance and the marketing of produce. A new concept emerged: that of the 'economically viable' peasant farmer, whose farm was likely to prosper, with a land surface of fewer than 12 h.r.b., and probably more than 5 h.r.b. (this minimum threshold was not explicitly mentioned, but it becomes apparent in the implementation of the programme). These thresholds are fixed in an empirical and arbitrary manner and do not correspond to any results of research or survey.

The second original feature resided in the fact that INDAP oriented and controlled the programme, but its experts and agronomists took no part in its actual implementation, which was subcontracted to private technical assistance firms approved by INDAP, and which were paid per family receiving technical assistance. The typical composition of an advisory unit in such firms was at least one technical manager, a veterinary surgeon and a secretary, plus three agronomists. 180 families would be advised by one unit. The concept of a homogeneous zone and the

INDAP Agricultural Development Plan for this zone was the same as for GTTs. The administrative side of the programme was well-defined: training, 12 group meetings a year for information purposes, and at least 10 visits a year for individual technical advice.

About 150 000 families were potential beneficiaries of this programme, the aim of INDAP being to cover 50 000 families within 10 years, and more than 13 000 in 1983–4. This target was far from being reached, as fewer than 20 000 families had benefited by 1988–9.

Towards a social policy (National Rural Development Plan and Basic Technological Transfer programme)

Neither the GTTs nor the PTTIs, which aimed at direct production efficiency and were concerned with only a restricted number of farms, were in a position to cope with the marginalisation of a significant part of peasant farming. On the contrary, it is quite obvious that they contributed to widening the technological gap. It was not until 1986 that an interdepartmental Commission for Rural Development was formed, to assess the situation and propose a Rural Development Plan which was to be approved in 1987. The aims were not clearly defined, but included improvement of the quality of life for the rural population. There resulted a series of measures connected with various aspects of rural life: health, education, communications, technical assistance for the most underprivileged, housing. The implementation of this programme was given over to the local political authorities (Regions, Provinces and Rural Districts), with an INDAP official being responsible for executive tasks. However, it was emphasised that this plan should rely on no supplementary budget but only on a redistribution of existing resources.

The Plan set up a specific programme as regards peasant farming: the Basic Technology Transfer programme (PTTB), in favour of farmers holding fewer than 5 h.r.b. These farmers having admittedly few prospects in the purely agricultural sector, support was also offered to the family and for training. The organisation follows the model of the PTTIs, the need being stressed of having women in the support teams, and training having to be in part oriented toward household tasks.

Although these peasant farmers represented the largest share of the rural population, INDAP admitted to helping no more than 7000 in 1988. Martner (1989) highlighted the fact that the aim of the PTTBs and of the Rural Development Plan was more to consolidate political support for the government than to solve the problems of peasant farming. Some preliminary solutions to these problems resulted from the action of many ONGs (Non-Governmental Organisations) often linked to the Church, which tried to fill the vacuum created by the withdrawal of government support from the needy (Gómez and Echeñique, 1988). ONGs aimed at coming to the aid of the poor, but they also intended to try and take up the challenge of the technical backwardness accumulated over decades by peasant farming. The experience acquired by ONGs was to prove very useful for the new administration coming to power in 1990.

8.3 THE POLICY OF THE AYLWIN GOVERNMENT

Priority of rural development

The new agricultural policy as defined by Minister Juan Agustín Figueroa resulted from the electoral programme of the Agricultural Commission of the '*Concertación Democrática*'. The agricultural weekly of the Mercurio Press Group, *Revista del Campo*, on 19 March 1991, described the main lines of this policy, less than a week after the new Minister took office. The title of the article is revealing in itself: 'Realism and Pragmatism'. Rural development is meant to touch, first and foremost, the social classes usually supported by INDAP. Priority is given to peasant farming, but without neglecting industrial farming, the importance of which is recognised as regards food supplies and export participation. 'Neither absolute free-traders nor absolute protectionists', therefore no questioning of the price policy or of the marketing of cereals. The budget limit fixed by the preceding government could be exceeded by calling on foreign aid and on the resources provided by the planned tax reform. This should allow the number of peasant farmers supported by INDAP to rise from 25 000 to 100 000 in 4 years. Rural development should also be able to benefit from other Departments: Education, Health, Housing, and Public Works, without this being merely a form of social aid, but rather oriented towards generation of an economic basis allowing the self-development of the under-privileged of the rural population.

Central role given to INDAP

Other statements by the Under-Secretary of State for Agriculture, Maximiliano Cox, and the head of INDAP, Hugo Ortega, together with the announcement of the new Budget in October 1990, defined the instruments and aims of this new policy. Technical backwardness is a specific trait of peasant farming, but it is regarded as a consequence rather than a cause. Action must be taken at several levels at the same time: technical training of the producer, technological transfer together with appropriate financing on the farm management level, and support by the state to infrastructure and assistance to farmers to organise the marketing of their produce. The 1991 Budget partly observed these priorities: a 16 per cent growth compared to 1990, but over 30 per cent rise in real value for the INDAP budget, centralising 62 per cent of the budget resources of the Ministry of Agriculture. An agreement was signed between the National Irrigation Commission, INDAP and FOSIS (Solidarity and Social Investment Fund) allowing peasant farmers to benefit from Law no. 18450 concerning irrigation. Subsidies reaching 75 per cent, or even 100 per cent for the poorest peasant farmers, are to be granted for small projects. In the South of the country, CORFO (the Development Corporation) approved a project aiming at the improvement of milk production and collection in favour of peasant farmers. An agreement was also to be entered upon between COTRISA, a cereal purchasing organisation, and INDAP to the benefit of peasant farmers, at the same time as INIA was going to direct part of its research effort towards the specific problems of peasant farming.

The limits of the subsidiary state

There are, however, some differences between theory and practice as regards these achievements and projects. INDAP, which had numbered up to 6000 officials between 1970 and 1973, has seen its staff dwindle to 800, among whom only 400 professional experts and technicians are to carry out a much more demanding new policy. Recruitment of extra staff is impossible, although the working budget is increasing.

The bulk of the work will be subcontracted to private technical assistance firms, as had been the case during the previous regime. Three types of problems arise: (1) that of the methods to be used and, specifically, the adaptation to the distinctive features of peasant farming production systems; (2) that of the training of the technicians employed by private technical assistance firms; and (3) that of the actual participation of peasant farmers themselves.

The questions of methods and training of technicians are to be dealt with by INDAP, which had become used to implementing 'top down" extension programmes addressed to the poor peasantry without any real analysis of the technical and economic functioning of farmers' production systems, and without any real participation from the farmers themselves.

Fortunately, research and development methods based on an analysis of peasant farming systems have already been applied experimentally by some ONGs on a limited scale, but which is nevertheless representative of the main agro-ecological types. These methods are borrowed from international research organisations, such as the farming system Research and Development methods of the French CIRAD (International Centre for Agronomical Research and Development), and farming system methods from the USA, Canada and other European countries.

One of these ONGs, Agraria, which is at present responsible for eight projects in different regions of the country, has already taken part in the intensive training of INDAP technicians. But not only the INDAP technicians must be trained, also those of the private technical assistance firms. It will also be necessary to find patterns common to different methods, which should allow an easier communication of information and needs between the targeted farmer and the instruments of development and research.

The private technical assistance firms and the ONGs are able to provide for these needs on a temporary basis, but it seems essential for the farmers themselves eventually to be able to take over, thus enabling them to negotiate directly with the State.

8.4 CONCLUSION

The relationships between the agricultural policies of the 1970s and 1980s and peasant farming in Chile can serve as a fairly good example to illustrate the remarks of Alain de Janvry (1986) on the interventions necessary to correct price policies:

> The main difficulty of any price policy is that the instruments are restricted and the aims are many. There are two solutions. The first consists in reducing the number of aims. This is, in substance, the neo-liberal solution. The second is to increase the number of instruments. Their diversification thus permits the prices to be used only in their most appropriate role: that of giving information as regards an effective allocation of resources *within a framework shaped by structural intervention*.

The policy followed during the first decade of the Pinochet regime allowed the price mechanism to be too powerful, entailing disastrous consequences for the food security of part of the population, together with a decline in the balance of trade as regards basic commodities, the dismantling of part of the agrifoodstuffs system (sugar refineries, flour-mills, dairy products), and above all an increasing marginalisation of peasant farming. A purely economic vision during the 1980s, separating economically viable agriculture from a social agriculture based on technical support programmes, only widened the existing gap, even if the outcome was favourable in production terms. The new administration of March 1990 seems to have accepted the importance of the problem posed by the marginalisation of peasant farming. Beyond the 'social debt' owed to this category of citizens which was mentioned in the '*Concertación Democrática*' programme, the real question is to mobilise the 'reserves of potential resources' and that is where difficulties arise, for Chile, like other Latin-American countries, is still firmly convinced of the superiority of large-scale industrial farming over peasant farming.

Notes

1. h.r.b.: *hectárea de riego básico* (basic Irrigated hectare: b.i.h.) One b.i.h. is the land area with productive capacity equivalent to an irrigated hectare of class I land in a district close to Santiago.

2. One must bear in mind that many investments had been made when Allende was in office or before, especially in irrigation and development of fruit farming.

References

Berry, R. A., Cline W. R. (1979) *Agrarian structure and Productivity in Developing Countries* (Baltimore and London: John Hopkins University Press).
De Janvry A. (1986) 'Sécurité alimentaire et intégration de l'agriculture: options et dilemmes', *CERES* vol. 19, no. 1 (January–February) pp. 33–7.
Díaz A. (1989) 'L'industrie chilienne au sortir de la crise,' *Problèmes d'Amérique Latine*, Notes et études documentaires, no. 4898, La documentation française (Paris) pp. 52–65.
Echeñique J. (1989) 'Les deux faces du boom agricole,' *Problèmes d'Amérique Latine*, Notes et études documentaires, no. 4898, La documentation française (Paris) pp. 66–4.
Echeñique J. and Rolando N. (1989) *'La Pequeña Agricultura. Una Reserva de Potencialidades y una Deuda Social,* (Santiago: Agraria).
Gómez S. and Echeñique J (1988) *'La Agricultura Chilena. Las Dos Caras de la Modernización',* (Santiago: FLACSO-Agraria).
Hurtado H., Valdés A. and Muchnik, E. (1990) *Trade, Exchange Rate, and Agricultural Pricing Policies in Chile* (Washington, D.C.: World Bank Comparative Studies) 2 vol.
Larraín B. (1989) 'Las instituciones agrarias en Chile: el ministerio de agricultura, apuntes de trabajo,' no. 11 (Santiago: GIA (Grupo de Investigaciones Agrarias)).
Martner G. (1989) *El hambre en Chile. Un estudio de la economía agroalimentaria nacional* (Santiago: GIA-UNRISD).
Revista del Campo, various numbers.
Rivera R. (1988) *Los campesinos chilenos* (Santiago: GIA (Grupo de Investigaciones Agrarias)).
Vio Grossi, F. (1990) *Resistencia campesina en Chile y en Mexico* (Santiago: Consejo de Educación de Adultos de America Latina (CEAAL) – Centro El Canelo de Nos).

9 Non-governmental Development Programmes for the Peasant Sector: A Critical Review

Julio A. Berdegué

9.1 INTRODUCTION

Peasants in Chile use half of the agricultural land, providing 30 per cent of the global national food supply, through the work of about 40 per cent of the total number of active workers in the agricultural sector.

The transfer of peasant owned lands to the capitalist sector, and the widening of the technological gap between these realities, have contributed to the decline in the relative importance of peasant production, even though the latter has shown modest rates of increase of production and productivity.

Per capita food availability decreased at least 20 per cent in the period of the military regime. Recovering the historical levels of food security will require a strong rate of growth in the national production of basic foodstuffs. Considering the actual and foreseeable limitations on the ability of capitalist agriculture to satisfy the eventual growth of food demand in a situation of democratisation, the peasant sector may regain a significant, even predominant role in feeding the country. Peasant production is today thus very important and it is possible that conditions favouring its expansion may arise in the future.

The subject of development guidelines and policies in the technological and productive dimension is considered a central issue by all relevant actors in the agricultural sector, although the alternatives proposed are varied. Awareness exists that, in the past, the country essentially limited itself to importing and applying, in a rather uncritical way, technological models with implicit and hidden features which ended up by obstructing and sometimes distorting the meaning, objectives and impact of de-

162

velopment programmes. The Pinochet government technological development programmes, and particularly those executed
under INDAP leadership, were meaningless in relation to the
dimensions of the peasant sector and the challenge of rural
development. Moreover, they suffered from an adherence to
basic concepts and methodological assumptions that the scientific community, in general, has since tended to abandon.

9.2 NON-GOVERNMENTAL PROGRAMMES

There are at least 60 non-governmental, non profit making organisations that are totally or partially concerned with rural development projects, in which there is usually some component of
support for peasant technological and productive development.

The first thing to be noted is the diversity and heterogeneity
among these Non-Governmental Organisations (NGOs), from
the viewpoint of their history, legal status, institutional organisation, specific objectives, methodology and size. It would be
difficult to try to give a thorough description of each one of these
NGOs (Gómez and Echeñique, 1988). Of 61 NGOs listed by
Gómez (1987), most were established after 1977, and 40 per cent
were set up only after 1983. The NGOs represent a reality that
has emerged due to the effects of the military regime's policies in
the countryside and on the production and living standards of
the peasantry. This in good measure explains both their virtues
and their defects and deficiencies.

The period when NGOs were born was the hardest in the
history of peasantry in recent years. It has been described as a
situation of marginalisation and progressive pauperisation of the
peasant sector. Even the global situation of the commercial
agricultural sector was marked by depression and economic
crisis, except in the agro-exporting subsector.

Most NGOs (44 out of 61) are regional agencies. They carry
out their work in a clearly defined geographical area, generally
equivalent to an administrative Region. Only 17 of the 61 NGOs
have 'nationwide' coverage, meaning that they carry out their
activities in several zones of the country. A group of 24 NGOs
are organisations directly depending on, or effectively run by
Church authorities, while the other 37 can be defined as private,
non-profit making agencies, though some of them maintain some

formal or informal relations with Church organisations.

In the late 1980s these NGOs employed almost 800 people, a number that was more or less equivalent to that of INDAP employees. Slightly over half of them had some training in agricultural sciences, while the rest were, mostly, specialists in the social sciences. More than half were professionals, while the rest possessed a technical level diploma or some training as field experts.

During 1986, four of these agencies functioned with a budget of over $180 000 and 11 of them with less than $36 000. The rest were in between these extremes.

Considering as beneficiaries only those families who received systematic support, some 15 000 peasant families benefited (i.e., participated in at least one of the several programmes of these agencies). This number increases if one includes sporadic and ocassional beneficiaries.

In general terms, these NGOs include among their activities training programmes, support of the local or regional peasant organisations, communications programmes, credit lines, technical assistance and the promotion of specific technological instruments or practices, generally of the 'organic', 'appropriate' or 'intermediate' kind. At the same time, a large number of NGOs include among their main objectives the promotion of values such as, for example, 'peasant dignity', solidarity, etc.

It is difficult to evaluate globally the real impact and quality of these programmes. First, because there are remarkable differences between them, when looked at individually: thus, some NGOs have won widespread acknowledgement for their work, while others provide clear examples of what should not be done in terms of rural development. Secondly, the diversity of aims and projects makes it difficult to define more or less general standards and parameters of evaluation.

Nevertheless, and assuming all the risks of a general conclusion when dealing with such a dissimilar universe, it can be said that, in terms of the technological and productive development of peasant agriculture, a high proportion of these NGOs performed (or perform?) work that ought to be described as inadequate and inefficient.

This negative global evaluation is particularly accurate, when actual achievements are matched against the assertion, that is often heard in the NGOs' environment, that their activities represent 'germs' or 'embryos' of a new development model for the peasantry, alternatives as much to the one proposed by the military regime as to those promoted in previous democratic periods.

Most of the peasant families participating in NGO programmes have not achieved production and living standards significantly different from those of their non-participant neighbours. Most programmes have unstable results. Results are sustained while the NGOs continue with their work and support plans, but they cannot be consolidated over time. They are unable to gain a space for self-affirmation, which is the basis for a new and higher scale of objectives and expectations.

In technological and productive matters, NGOs tend to get involved, *a priori*, with models and proposals that often bear little relation to the peasants' real interests and problems. Worse, there are cycles of 'fashions', during which, and for as long as they last, a large proportion of NGOs give high priority to a certain technology or methodology, 'cliché' or specific practice, to the exclusion of everything else: 'high beds', 'composting', 'participative diagnosis', aquaculture, and 'integrated farms', are examples around which real crusades have been organised; these usually end as quickly as they have begun.

Donor agencies share responsibility for promoting these tendencies to oscillate and improvise, that have made it difficult to generate technological proposals that may be effectively promoted with stability and that have a minimum level of coherence with the objectives, characteristics and real needs and restrictions of peasant agriculture. The NGOs, in general, pay little attention to evaluating short- and long-term trends in agriculture, which makes it difficult to redefine their policies and objectives in order to face new challenges arising from changes in the rural and national reality.

Perhaps as a result of the period in which they were created and of the place they occupy within the rural world, there is a tendency to occupy a marginal space, restricted to the 'alternative area', with a limited capacity for broad and open interrelations with all the actors in the agricultural sector.

Of course, the possibility of establishing connecting bridges with a wider world depends not only and exclusively on the will of the NGOs, for the reproduction of the authoritarian and excluding model of the military regime was strongly marked in the rural sector.

For example, in early 1989 the CRATE foundation, run by the Talca Catholic Bishopric, was excluded by an arbitrary government decision from participation in INDAP's Integral Technological Transference Programme, in which it had acted as a Consultant Enterprise. In this way, not only was the access to technical and financial support for 300 families affected, but one of the few spaces of collaboration between state institutions and non-governmental organisations was cut off.

This occupation of a marginal space produces a sort of immovility, or at least slowness to respond to the challenges raised by the government's initiatives in terms of rural development – as, for example, with the National Rural Development Plan. Likewise, a significant number of NGOs took a long time before taking into account the modifications seen in the agrarian sector after the definition of the new policies of price support for internal food production, implemented since the breakdown of the neo-liberal free-market model in 1982–3. As a result, peasants linked to NGOs have also seen the technological and productive gap with the medium-sized and large properties grow.

Some agrarian analysts, observing those tendencies, argue – and not without justification – that the NGOs' style and orientations consecrate the marginality of peasant production, by being unable to respond dynamically to new challenges raised by the process of modernisation of capitalist agriculture.

Another negative element is the NGOs' lack of skill in articulating and co-ordinating programmes and policies among themselves, with a view not only to making better use of available resources, but to reinforcing their proposal and intermediation capacity with the whole of society, and particularly with the rural world.

There are some zones of the country where a significant number of NGOs are operating. They have accumulated vast experience in their work with particular sectors of the peasantry. That is the case with, for example, the IX Region, where over a dozen NGOs carry out support programmes aimed at Mapuche communities, and where it would be perfectly feasible to design a global development proposal for this peasant sector. The same applies in the VIII Region, where there is also an important concentration of efforts, but not co-ordination of them.

These critical comments do not apply to each and every NGO. Also, many of the difficulties indicated originate partially in the social, political, economic and cultural conditions imposed by the military regime. Alternative institutions, with democratic principles, as is the case with NGOs, may not reach full development and deploy all their potentialities and capacities in the context of the authoritarian and excluding model of the military regime. In this sense, and other things being equal, the prospects for valuable NGO work during the 1990s look very good.

We may now try to state what, in our judgement, are the most noticeable aspects in the rural NGOs' experience, the previous warning about difficulties and vagueness inherent to any general conclusions being equally valid here.

First, it ought to be noted as positive that there are a significant number of NGOs representing, with all their limitations, the will to define ways of rural and peasant development distinct from those promoted by the military regime and its institutions.

The accumulated experience of these years is a valuable capital. The country is in a better position to define rural development policies that are both equitable and efficient, after considering the mistakes and successes of the NGOs. It cannot but be impressive, for example, that in the late 1980s the NGOs employed as many persons and attended as many peasant families as INDAP, covering almost all the administrative Regions.

Secondly, it is a matter of consensus among NGOs that rural development must be subjected to the principles of decentralisation and local participation, as a means of effectively affecting living and production standards in the peasant sector. The methodological experiences based on these NGO principles are very diverse, and have in their actual operation demonstrated both the defects and virtues of this approximation to a definition of the rural development problem.

Thirdly, the efforts of many NGOs to articulate the different dimensions of rural development into a one single action are praiseworthy. Combination of efforts in technical assistance, training, local monitors and leaders' education, promoting organisation, credit, housing and health care, etc. foreshadow a scheme that seems to be more valuable than those that divided these diverse themes into so many other agencies and bureaucracies.

Finally, NGOs have tried, with all their limitations, to

redefine paradigms and parameters of rural development, questioning the policy profile, addressed as it was exclusively towards the obtaining of economic results, and the mechanical identity between development and modernity. In many cases, the initiative in re-thinking and revitalising rural development has been in the hands of NGOs. This was particularly important considering that many official efforts were still subjected to the same theoretical concepts as in the 1960s and 1970s. To a certain extent, NGOs have been able to put forward the relevant *questions* regarding the definition of rural development policies, although there are still obvious deficiencies in terms of finding accurate and feasible *answers*. These answers should not only be 'correct'; they should also be capable of becoming 'operational'.

References

Gómez, S. (1987) 'Organismos Privados de Desarrollo Rural en Chile: Algunas características Básicas,' in *Seminario Nacional Experiencias de Desarrollo Rural.* Area de Pastoral Social (Santiago: Conferencia Episcopal de Chile).

Gómez, S. and Echeñique, J. (1988) *La Agricultura Chilena: Las Dos Caras de la Modernización* (Santiago: FLACSO Agraria).

10 Self-help Organisations and Non-governmental Programmes of Rural Development

Rigoberto Rivera

The purpose of this chapter is to examine the origins and development of self-help organisations (SHOs). These organisations exist in order to supplement the cash incomes or the amount of self-produced consumer goods available to the poor in the countryside and villages. Our analysis is undertaken, on the one hand, within the general framework of the social and economic development of poor sectors in the Chilean countryside, villages and small urban centers linked to agricultural activity and, on the other, in the context of the production and social development activities being carried out by Non-Governmental Organisations (NGOs).

10.1 THE CONTEXT OF AGRARIAN CHANGE AND THE PROBLEM OF POVERTY

The Pinochet regime policies contributed to a situation of increasing poverty in the agrarian sector that resulted in the emergence of a new social group: those displaced from agriculture who, having nowhere to go, set up precarious dwellings around towns and in peasant areas. We have called this social sector '*pobladores rurales*', (landless rural inhabitants or 'rural shanty town dwellers') because their most important characteristic is a situation of great social and economic marginality in the fringe between rural and urban areas. These rural poor, together with smallholders, make up the bulk of the poor population involved in agriculture. Their most common employment situation is temporary work. A central protagonist is now the '*temporero*' or temporary worker (Rivera and Cruz, 1984).

169

This Chilean situation of rural poverty and a new type of marginal settlement, corresponding to a style of capitalist development based on casual employment, is not unique. It is possible to find similar labour patterns and population settlements in several countries in Latin America. In this labour scheme of predominantly unstable employment participate both small holding peasants who are typically used as seasonal manpower, and landless temporary workers, who are inserted in the labour market throughout the year.

This is the social context in which self-help organisations were created. In the following sections we shall describe the main results of research carried out in 1986–7 by the Santiago Agrarian Research Group (Grupo de Investigaciones Agrarias, GIA), in collaboration with the Centre for Research on Latin America and the Caribbean (CERLAC), of York University, Toronto, Canada. By way of conclusion some ideas towards self-criticism of the work attempted by GIA and other NGOs are presented in the last section.

10.2   SELF-HELP ORGANISATIONS

The study covered 230 predominantly rural communes (or municipalities), between the provinces of Petorca and Chiloé, in Chile's central agrarian region.

A total of 193 self-help organisations aimed at generating incomes, either directly through self-consumption or through selling. In some cases they may also carry out some form of community services, as is the case of the community first-aid chests. These SHOs had a total of 3946 members. The projection of these figures to the whole universe indicates that the existing organisations in the zone studied should be about 1500 to 2500. The average number of members is 20 per SHO who, also in a global projection, should amount to a total of between 30 000 and 50 000 members. Approximately 25 per cent of the members participate with their spouses. Around 5 per cent of poor families participate in some SHO. This proportion is significantly lower than the 15 per cent membership of similar organisations detected by a similar study carried out in Santiago (Hardy, 1987a; 1987b).

In any case, these figures do not adequately show the relative importance of SHOs. Membership is lower than that of trade unions (50 000 members in 1988), but much higher than that of cooperatives (8000 members in 1984) (Molina and Rivera, 1984). These membership figures are not exclusive, for there are a number of SHOs that are part of bigger organisations, especially trade unions. There is also a proportion of people simultaneously participating in SHOs and in the peasant movement's organisations.

10.3   AGRARIAN CHANGE, POVERTY AND SELF-HELP ORGANISATIONS

The actual model of agricultural development has stressed regional differences. Thus, some zones can be identified with exporting activities (fruit growing and forestry), exhibiting fast economic growth, while other regions with annual crops are orientated towards the internal market (mixed crops, grains and cattle). For many years the prevailing situation in the latter was one of stagnation or crisis. In these regions is also concentrated the bulk of the peasant population. Whereas in the export-based regions the predominant tendency is towards proletarianisation, in others there is rather an increment in the number of peasants, together with a decline in the availability of land per family.

Such differences generate contrasting social and economic effects in each region. Different forms of expression of poverty are present. In some zones, peasant pauperisation prevails. In others, there is a great development of temporary employment. At the same time, there are zones with a large number of women in wage work (the fruit growing zone), while there are others (forestry zones) where there are no possibilities of taking on female workers. All this is reflected in the relative importance of SHOs and in their specific characteristics.

In the annual crop regions there is an average of 15 SHOs per commune, in the fruit growing ones there are only 5, and in the forestry regions, 9. In the mixed crop regions there is a strong relationship between rural poverty and the crisis in peasant agriculture.

In the fruit growing and forestry regions most of the members of SHOs are wage earners (75 per cent); in those of mixed crops and cattle raising, smallholding peasants prevail.

An examination of the specific activities of organisations in each productive region shows that they are consistent with regional characteristics. Activities are of the most varied kind, and respond to the diverse compelling needs faced by some social layers of a community or neighbourhood: income generation, production of food, housing, clothing, health, access to credit, training, agrarian production, etc. In several villages community soup kitchens for families living in extreme poverty, children and elderly people are active. Many workshops do not sell their products, but they are consumed by the members themselves. Other workshops help poor sectors of the community, for instance, they provide clothing for school-age children.

In the fruit growing region there is a predominance of workshops (craft production and mending second-hand clothes), and service organisations (housing). In the forestry region there are more clothing repair groups than productive workshops, which reflects a situation of greater poverty. In the farming regions there are also many workshops (in villages), but peasant committees, vegetable garden committees and health groups dominate quantitatively and offer a higher profile.

Another aspect considered was the degree of urbanisation in those places where SHOs were located. But location is also related to the type of region. The SHOs in urban areas are mostly located in the forestry region, which is noted for the strong shift away from peasant characteristics due to the appearance of massive forestry plantations. In the fruit growing regions, SHOs are more or less evenly distributed between towns, villages and rural zones. In the mixed crops and cattle raising zones, most of the organisations are located in rural areas. Most of the workshops are located in towns, while the peasants' committees are rural. The vegetable garden committees, on the other hand, are distributed among all three locations (rural, villages and towns).

In terms of the gender composition of SHOs, there are some well-defined tendencies. Women are a majority, totalling 2549 members (64.4 per cent of the total); 107 organisations were composed solely of women. In other 37 predominantly male organisations, widows also participated, and 43 SHOs had family groups as their organisational basis.

Men tend to be predominant in those organisations operating in the agricultural production area – such as peasants' committees – while women were predominant in practically all the others, particularly in workshops.

10.4   NGOs AND ORGANISATIONAL DEVELOPMENT

Self-help organisations have developed in a complex environment of multiple relations with development support institutions (NGOs) and with the peasant movement's organisations (trade unions, cooperatives and federations). One of the surprises in the study was the fact that SHOs were largely unable to maintain the organisation itself and to generate the necessary resources to carry out their activities by themselves. It was found that those NGOs engaged in support to peasants had a fundamental role to play in creating and developing SHOs. In relation to the specific type of help, 64 per cent of the groups received support in the form of raw materials, and 18 per cent were receiving credits. Other help consisted of food and clothing (14 per cent), technical assistance (50 per cent), and legal assistance (15 per cent). Several SHOs received two or more types of assistance, in some cases from different NGOs. There were also some formally different groups, but with almost the same membership, with different activities and linked to different NGOs.

Out of 193 SHOs, 152 were linked to the Catholic Church, and 21 were connected to lay or protestant NGOs. Only 20 SHOs did not rely on basic support from a NGO.

The gender differences in membership seem to be related to the history of peasant organisations and to the support systems. Men are predominant in organisations without any support and in those supported by technical assistance NGOs. Most of these organisations derive from former unions or peasant committees developed during the land reform period. Women are predominant in organisations tied to traditional church institutions: in the latter the composition is: 3 per cent men; 75 per cent women and 22 per cent families.

In relation to formal integration to more complex organisational structures, there is a number of SHOs affiliated to some other organisation in the peasant movement. Almost a quarter are affiliated to trade unions, peasants' associations and cooperatives. This affiliation does not involve significant direct support, even though they receive legal assistance, training, and specific contacts with NGOs furnishing direct support through loans, technical assistance, and so on. There were other links with local community organisations, political parties, local government, and others.

10.5   SELF-HELP ORGANISATIONS AND NGOs IN RURAL DEVELOPMENT

NGOs are especially important because they obtain and channel in a systematic way resources allowing SHOs to carry out their activities. The latter, once created, ask for support from the NGOs in order to gain access to resources which the members do not possess and that are essential to achieve their objectives.

In some cases, the NGOs themselves create organisations with groups of peasants. In order to do this, they generally operate through historical leaders (from old co-ops or trade unions), or with those of the local Christian communities, or rank and file political leaders.

There are basically two types of NGOs: those more closely linked to the pastoral work of a Church (Catholic or Protestant), such as CARITAS, IMPRU, etc. which mainly organise women's workshops; and those concerned with rural technical assistance and the promotion of productive organisations of peasant smallholders. In the case of the Catholic Church, these development actions precede agrarian reform. The NGOs of a more technical character appeared in the late 1970s. They started to operate through agrarian development technicians who were formerly civil servants, dismissed in or immediately after 1973.

NGOs operate within a development paradigm stressing the NGOs' and SHOs' development potential, small-scale development, popular education, and self-diagnosis techniques, which can be inserted into global concepts such as 'the other development' and 'development on a human scale'. These approaches prevailed in the 1980s.

Because of their concept of development, and attitude towards profitability, NGOs differ from state and capitalist enterprises. Their development actions cannot be perceived merely as production projects. The NGOs' working methods favour the training, organisation, and self-development of peasants. NGOs define as priorities the social liberation and dignification of the rural poor.

NGOs aim at the creation of active social subjects in the community. But rural poverty has consolidated a system of income generation which encourages men to seek paid work outside the community; thus, a predominance of women can be observed in SHOs. This situation poses several questions about the capability of this NGO development model to generate better living conditions for the rural poor. The low male participation is related to labour migration, but also to the perceived low ability of SHOs to generate sufficient incomes to maintain a bigger male participation. There are also questions about the dependence–autonomy balance in SHOs.

At least partly, the problems of lack of autonomy seem to depend on the male–female relationship within the household. There is no positive disposition of the men to allow their wives to participate in these organisations. A significant proportion of women were not able to participate in SHOs because of their husbands' opposition.

Studying these variables is very important in order to obtain information regarding the organisations' efficiency. Elements such as labour market dynamics, and annual employment–unemployment trends and fluctuations, are significant for the participation in SHOs, especially by women. In the fruit growing region, the expansion of female work has implied crisis and the disappearance of workshops and other income generation groups.

After several years of activity, technical NGOs are searching for new paths in order more rationally to take advantage of the development resources available. So far, they have not succeeded in promoting economic organisations capable of functioning autonomously. In this particular sense, the NGO development model has failed.

NGOs are starting to become aware of the problems of their approach to rural development, and aware that they are misusing the resources available. They admit that they lack theoretical and methodological instruments, as well as a broader concept of development on which their action could be based. Many of these problems were brought to light in the NGOs' National Seminar, in Santiago in July 1987. In this seminar, the NGOs' deficiencies were grouped under ten headings: (1) lack of coordination; (2) lack of evaluation methods; (3) lack of diagnosis; (4) lack of identification of the purposes of the NGOs; (5) lack of proper knowledge of local conditions and of the peasants' demands; (6) 'ivory tower' programmes with no connection with reality; (7) lack of systematisation and socialisation of experiences; (8) stressing production while disregarding commercialisation; (9) stressing organisation for its own sake; and (10) low profitability of the productive projects.

Our own impression is that the NGOs have well articulated theories, but that these institutions find it difficult to put these principles into practice in actual development actions. In fact, several inconsistencies appear between the theoretical model and the reality in the countryside. These two spheres cannot be adequately related to each other in order to reach a high level of efficiency in rural development. Perhaps the answer is to look for new methods of development more closely related to the actual rural social structure, and less to Utopian models based on a romantic notion of peasant solidarity and co-operation.

References

Hardy, Clarissa (1987a) 'Pobreza y estrategias de supervivencia: Desafíos metodológicos del futuro', in Urzua, R. and Dooner, P. (eds), *La opción preferencial por los pobres. De la teoría a la práctica* (Santiago: CISOC-Bellarmino).

Hardy, Clarissa (1987b) 'Organizarse para vivir. Pobreza urbana y organización popular' (Santiago: PET).

Molina, R. and Rivera, R. (1984) 'Las organizaciones campesinas en Chile (catastro 1984)' (Santiago: GIA, Working Document).

Rivera, R. and Cruz, M. E. (1984) *Pobladores Rurales. Cambios en el Poblamiento y el Empleo Rural en Chile* (Santiago: GIA).

11 Continuity, Legitimacy, and Agricultural Development: Conclusions

David E. Hojman

This chapter aims at bringing together the principal conclusions of the volume, emphasising some particular aspects and questions. Policy continuity in relation to the late 1980s was rightly defined by the Aylwin government policymakers as an essential instrument for further agricultural growth. But in a democratic environment the Aylwin policies, in part precisely because of their strong element of continuity, could be implemented only if they were perceived as legitimate by the majority of the rural population, and by the poor in particular. This means that substantial improvements in agricultural income distribution, and in the quantity and quality of the social services provided to the rural poor, were unavoidable. In order to achieve legitimacy it was, and is, necessary to introduce changes. A lucid, creative combination of continuity and change was the only guarantee of success for the Aylwin policies, and for those of future democratic administrations. Continuity and legitimacy are the fundamental pillars for democratic agricultural development.

Chilean agriculture in the 1990s presents features which are completely different from those observed 25 or 30 years ago. The processes of land reform and counter-reform definitively eliminated the 'structural bottlenecks' described by structuralist academics. The typical farm is now medium-sized, the land exploitation uses modern methods, farmers respond to signals provided by the price system, and the country is a net exporter of agricultural products. The agricultural trade balance (including forestry, but not industrial products based on forestry activities) moved from a deficit of $500 million in 1981 to a surplus of the same amount in 1988, and of almost $2000 million in 1991. All this does not mean that there are no problems any more. Some

177

problems from the past remain, and new problems have appeared, in some cases precisely as a result of success. Arguments have been exchanged as to whether homogeneity or heterogeneity is the principal sign of these transformations in the countryside. But this discussion is somewhat redundant: there is homogeneity in the sense that there is rapid advancement towards capitalist development in agriculture, and also heterogeneity in that this development occurs at a very different pace in particular sectors, regions and even products.

Perhaps the most noticeable aspect of the Aylwin agrarian policies is how similar they are to Pinochet's in the late 1980s. The Minister of Agriculture is a farmer and a member of the moderate Radical Party. The Under-Secretary, Maximiliano Cox, played an important role in academic studies upon which the new policies were based. Cox and other officials trained either abroad or in NGOs. They represent a new generation in relation to the Allende period. Policy continuity in relation to the 1980s is apparent in land tenure, price regimes, exchange rates, interest rates, and treatment of foreign capital. Attempts at achieving legitimacy can be seen in the changes to the 1979 Labour Law, higher minimum wages, new social programmes (for instance in rural housing), and new projects for technical assistance and credit to peasants. Producer price stability is guaranteed for several items. Access to credit by commercial farmers at low but positive interest rates is possible. Farmers' debts are being renegotiated. However, the creation of a system of deposits for short-term foreign loans in 1991, with the purpose of improving stability of these financial flows, will increase the cost of credit to farmers and fruit exporters who use these loans. On the other hand, the large amount of resources accumulated by the privately run pension funds (*Administradoras de Fondos Previsionales*, AFPs) means that there is no shortage of domestic savings to finance profitable investment projects (Hojman, 1990a, 1992).

11.1   MACROECONOMIC BALANCE AND THE IMPORTANCE OF POLICY

Macroeconomic balance is as important as any specific policies for the rural sector. This includes the control of inflation and preserving a stable and realistic exchange rate. Labour costs have increased, but it is unlikely that they will eventually constitute a serious problem for exporters. The irrigation and transport infrastructures are being improved, but possibly not as rapidly as necessary, and some bottlenecks may be inevitable. Possibly more attention should also be paid to ecological concerns. The income elasticity of domestic demand for basic foodstuffs is possibly quite high (Hojman, 1990b). This high elasticity, together with general recovery of the economy after anti-inflationary adjustment (according to preliminary estimates, GDP grew at a rate of 6 per cent in 1991, and a 6.5 per cent rate is expected for 1992), and some redistribution of income towards groups with a higher marginal propensity to consume, suggest that the state of relative stagnation affecting the production of basic foodstuffs during many years in the 1970s and the 1980s will not be repeated in the first half of the 1990s.

Let us now return to one of the questions inspired by Patricio Silva's Chapter 4 in this volume. At some stage, the 'traditional landowners' of the 1960s became the 'dynamic entrepreneurs' of the 1980s and 1990s. How, why, and when did this happen? Who or what changed? Rural entrepreneurs, academics, or society? Maybe all of them? Any simple explanation may be far from complete. Possibly, individuals with the potential to become highly dynamic entrepreneurs were always there but, before the land reform period, they were engaged in activities in which rewards were much better than in agriculture. In a rent-seeking society, characterised by high rates of protection to some domestic activities, they were likely to have been effective rent-seekers, in more or less the same way in which, in a socialist regime, they would have been fast-track members of the government party apparatus, or successful black market operators. Over the long term, the final responsibility for how individuals act and what they become lies with education. But in a shorter-term perspective, it may all depend upon policy. As to social scientists, they may have failed to see the entrepreneurs (or potential entrepreneurs) before, not because the latter were not there, but because there was no room for them in the social scientists' theoretical models. It is most unlikely that the recent academic interest among progressive Chilean intellectuals in entrepreneurs and businessmen (Gómez and Echeñique, 1986; Cruz, 1988; Montero, 1990) results from the fact that these entrepreneurs and businessmen suddenly appeared from nowhere. Rather, attention is being paid now to social and economic actors who have always been there, because only recently have the intellectuals changed their theoretical models, and now there is room in them for actors who previously were seen only as parasites, soon about to be swept away, thrown into history's dustbin. The essential continuity between the 'traditional landowners' and the 'new entrepreneurs' is apparent in the fact that the 'old landowner' Jorge Prado, a key Minister of Agriculture in the Pinochet regime, was re-elected as Chairman of the National Farmers' Association (SNA) in 1991.

The key issue here is the all-important role of policy. The links going from behaviour to theory to policy, and back to behaviour again, may constitute vicious or virtuous circles. The wrong policies generate patterns of anti-social behaviour, patterns which suggest hypotheses for theoretical interpretation which, if accepted, are bound to reinforce these incorrect policies and behavioural patterns. The only place in practice where a vicious circle can be broken is at the policy stage. The history of Chilean agriculture is full of examples of this type of vicious circle, as well as examples of how a basically correct policy, and the certainty that this policy will be maintained, generate a favourable outcome. Fruit exports, forestry, beetroot farming, and many others could all be used to illustrate this point. We should not be surprised that a Chilean agriculture predominantly based on free markets and private initiative, in an overwhelmingly open economy, is such a huge success. That this should happen had already been predicted in the 1960s (Schultz, 1968).

11.2   THE INTERNATIONAL ECONOMY, THE UNITED STATES, AND QUALITY CONTROL

The Aylwin government aimed at increasing exports from 30 per cent of output in 1989 to 35 per cent in 1993–4. As GDP is expected to expand at a rate of 5 per cent per year, this means export growth of more than 40 per cent in 4 years. Remarkable as this is, Chilean exports will still be modest in relation to those from Singapore or Taiwan. The country's popularity as an agricultural exporter is as large as that as a recipient of direct foreign investment. Two mechanisms, DL600 and Chapter 19, have made it possible, respectively, to grant foreign investors the same treatment as domestic ones, and to reduce substantially the external debt. As a share of GDP, foreign investment in Chile has been the largest in Latin America since 1989. Between the first half of 1990 and the first half of 1991, actual direct foreign investment remained stable, but new authorisations (which should materialise after some time lags) rose by 20 per cent. Investment is addressed to those sectors with the highest comparative advantage, which to a large extent means agriculture and forestry. Conditions of soil, climate, location in the southern hemisphere, economic, political, institutional, educational and cultural, give Chile immense comparative advantages in international markets.

But specific conditions in individual markets require careful study. The United States imported 20 per cent of total Chilean exports in 1989, but much more of some key items. Relations with the USA are crucial to the export strategy. In this sense, practically all the problems inherited from the 1980s have been solved: the exclusion of Chile from the Generalised System of Preferences (GSP) and the Overseas Private Investment Corporation (OPIC) insurance system for American investment abroad; the Kennedy Amendment banning exports of US arms; and the legal questions concerning the murder of Orlando Letelier, a Minister in Allende's cabinet, in Washington in the 1970s. The only remaining problem is that of protectionism in the USA, reflected, for instance, in the 'marketing orders'. These are temporary, seasonal-only quality controls applied in the USA to both domestic and imported produce. They affect table grapes, and it has been proposed to extend them to paw-paws, pistachios, kiwis, peaches, plums and apples. Because Chilean fruit supply to the US market is counter-seasonal, the effect of the 'marketing orders' is not critical, but Chilean exporters see them as representing a dangerous protectionist precedent. On the positive side, Chile is the most enthusiastic supporter in Latin America of the Bush initiative to create a free market in the Western Hemisphere. As a trading partner Chile will never be as important as Mexico for the USA, but Chile and Mexico negotiated their own bilateral free trade agreement, which came in force on January 1, 1992.

Often protectionist moves hide behind quality control arguments. There is no agreement between Chilean producers as to what to do in order to improve the quality of fruit exports. Some argue that quality enhancement is the best tactic against protectionism, with the added advantage that it would reduce supplies and increase prices. But this view is contested by lower quality producers (*rastrojeros*). Proposals for government intervention have been rejected. Possibly this intervention is not really necessary, since concentration at the exporting stage leaves large shippers in the position of effectively becoming quality controllers. This was observed in the 1990–1 season, in which the quality of shipments to the USA was considerably higher than in 1989–90. Unfortunately some lower quality fruit was deviated towards European markets. Fruit exports in volume increased by 10 per cent in the 1990–1 season, in relation to a year before. This was made up of an 18 per cent decline in exports to the USA, and a 35 per cent increase in exports to Europe.

In other products quality control has been reached more easily. After the sorbitol episode, which meant that large quantities of Chilean wine had to be withdrawn from European markets because they exceeded the EC approved sorbitol limits, the Chilean government modified the law and adopted the EC sorbitol limits as its own.

11.3   FRUIT, FORESTRY, WINE AND OTHER EXPORTS

The key word here is 'other'. It is true that partly because of concentration in the American market and in apples and table grapes, and assuming that quality is kept constant, apple and table grape physical exports can be significantly increased only if producers are prepared to see their prices fall. But on the other hand rumours of death of the non-traditional export drive have been greatly exaggerated. The political transition from Pinochet to Aylwin did not affect the dynamism of these exports; far from it: agricultural and fisheries exports rose by 10 per cent between the first half of 1990 and the first half of 1991 (this does not include cellulose, paper and fishmeal which are classified as industrial; industrial exports grew by 17 per cent). Fruits such as pears, plums, peaches, oranges, lemons, avocados and apricots offer an unexploited potential. The same applies to greens and vegetables: onions, asparagus, garlic, tomatoes, melons, radishes, oregano, artichokes, peppers, broccoli, sweet corn, endives, sweet potatoes, cauliflowers, spinach, turnips, parsnips, swedes, courgettes, sweetbread, miniature corn, mushrooms and so on. Orchard garden produce is highly labour intensive, it requires low capital investment, and it allows producers to change from item to item on an annual basis according to market fluctuations. Livestock exports include many lines, from rabbit to offal. Pacts agreed in 1991 allow the free entry of Chilean kiwis to Japan, custard apples and by 1993 tomatoes to the US, and a number of fruits and vegetables to Canada. Other accords have also been reached to establish quality control systems by the importer at the point of harvesting and packing rather than at the point of destination.

There seems to be general agreement that for a long time subsidies to forestry have been far too generous. They may have encouraged both excessive firm concentration and environmental decline, as well as making the plight of poor peasants in forestry regions even worse. However, the growth in the contribution to exports by the forestry sector is so dramatic that the Aylwin government may have decided to tamper at the margins, rather than change the subsidy structure completely. Apart from establishing some programmes of support to poor peasants, the subsidy allocated to the plantation of native trees was increased (as opposed to that granted to radiata pine and eucaliptus). The process of authorisation of new projects also reflects a new concern for the native forest. Exports increase regularly, year after year. Expansion between the first half of 1990 and the first half of 1991 was 4 per cent (this again does not include industrial products of forestry origin, which expanded much faster).

In principle, Chile is in the position of being able to produce some of the best wines in the world. This has been confirmed by the investment policies of winemakers of international standing such as the Catalonian firm Miguel Torres, Rothschild of Chateau Lafite fame, the Californian Franciscan Vineyards, and others. These foreign investors will produce only or mainly for external markets, since local consumers are unlikely to pay their prices, despite the fact that these prices are ridiculously small by international standards. Given the low cost of production in Chile, the only concern here is to improve quality. The cost of land as compared with, for example, Bordeaux, is negligible. With adequate quality the potential is limitless. At the beginning of 1990, two Chilean wines were chosen by the magazine *Wine Spectator* as the best buy of the quarter in the American market. The respective producer increased sales that year by a factor of seven. But even after this expansion its sales became only 10 per cent of those of the largest Chilean exporter to the US market. US consumers drink four litres of wine per year, against 30 litres drank by Chileans, and 70 litres by the French. The potential for growth in the American market is thus spectacular, even if Chilean wine is unlikely ever to take the largest share of the US market away from Californian wine.

A similar picture appears in the European Community. Chilean wines will never be able to control as large a share of the market in Great Britain as Australian wines do, or as large a share of the local markets as local wines in France, Germany, Italy or Spain. But Chilean wines still won first prizes in the International Wine Fair of Bordeaux in 1989, 1990 and 1991. Total wine exports rose by 66 per cent between January and May 1991, in relation to the same period in the previous year. This includes 90 per cent growth in wholesale (unbottled) and 93 per cent growth in sparkling wine.

Exports of semi-manufactures and simple manufactures are just beginning but they show great dynamism. They include conserves, juices, beer, spirits and liqueurs, jams and marmalades, chocolate, sweets and other sugar products, pasta, dry onions and garlic, tomato paste, dry yeast, furniture, wooden toys, floral arrangements, and even sticks for ice cream, spiders and lizards.

11.4   PROTECTION GRANTED TO DOMESTIC AGRICULTURE AND AGRO-INDUSTRY

Does it make sense to pay any cost in order to achieve self-sufficiency in food production? This question was raised by several authors in this volume, and in particular by Robert Gwynne and Anna Bee in Chapter 5. When the IANSA sugar beet programme was designed in 1982, for purposes of estimation of its internal rate of return it was assumed that the international price of sugar would be 17 cents per pound (Valdivia, 1988). This is the equivalent of 374 dollars per ton. This assumption proved to be highly unrealistic. The only occasions when the price has reached this level were in 1974–5, and in 1980–1, in both cases at least partly as a result of the oil booms. Sugar refining and sugar transport are energy intensive. But the sugar price collapsed much faster than the oil price. By 1984 the price of sugar was down to 5 cents. A price band was established by the Chilean government in the 1983–4 season, aimed at reducing the fluctuations in the domestic price to only about a third of the wild swings in the world market. But this by itself was insufficient as protection against cheaper imports, and the government was forced to establish a specific tariff on sugar imports, to be charged on top of the general tariff applicable to all imports, which was then 15 per cent.

The Chilean economic authorities were not the only ones to commit this large forecasting error. The Inter American Development Bank (IDB) in 1986 was predicting a world sugar price of 391 dollars per ton in 1989, and an average annual price of 571 dollars for the period 1990–2000. However, this prediction was swiftly corrected in their 1987 report. The forecast was reduced to only 211 dollars for 1989, and 201 dollars for 1990–2000 (Inter American Development Bank, 1986; 1987). The question, however, is not only one of forecasting accuracy. Some people are prepared to argue that the social benefit of being self-sufficient in food is worth paying a high price (for further discussion see Chapters 3 and 4 by Shanti Chakravarty and Patricio Silva in this volume). Many countries protect their domestic food (and sugar) producing industries almost regardless of cost. Maximiliano Cox, who in the late 1980s led the team in charge of designing the agricultural programme of the Aylwin government, deleted a reference to beet sugar in the final version of their report (Cox and Chateauneuf, 1988). The reference, which appears only in the preliminary version, is: 'according to a study requested by the World Bank, IANSA's are the most efficient sugar beet processing plants, and some of the most efficient sugar operations (including cane based ones), in the world' (Cox, 1988, p. 28). But this is highly misleading, and Cox was right in deleting it. High yields in Chilean beet growers and low unit costs in IANSA plants are meaningless if the domestic industry can survive only behind high tariff barriers against cheaper foreign competition.

Even if the central purpose of the sugar beet programme was to create employment, there were, and are, cheaper ways of subsidising the creation of new jobs. In the most favourable case, the programme has been responsible for the creation of about 30 000 jobs. This assumes that without the programme no alternative work would have been available for up to 15 000 rural labourers and industrial workers and for another 15 000 small and medium-size farmers. This is possibly a realistic assumption in the short run, but it becomes increasingly un-realistic as the planning horizon expands. The most conservative estimate of the social cost of the programme is represented by the specific tariff, 150 dollars per ton in the late 1980s. Since about 300 000 tons were produced every year, the total annual cost amounted to 45 million dollars. The implicit subsidy (in the form of higher prices paid by consumers) required to generate each new job is thus 1500 dollars per year. This is far too expensive, more than three times the subsidy necessary to create new jobs in alternative programmes (Coloma, 1987). Employment creation should be supported, but subsidies should go where they are most effective. This is more likely to be in exportables than in import-substitution activities (Corbo and Meller, 1982).

Moreover, there may be other social costs of the beet pro-gramme. Not only poor quality, non-irrigated coastal land is used by it, but also some high quality land in the Central Valley. High protection may be artificially keeping in business beet operations which should make way and release resources for other, more productive uses. Also, the high domestic price of sugar represents an artificially high item of cost for potential exporters of non-traditional products and manufactures. The beet programme has shown that, given the proper incentives and techniques, even the poorest peasant in the most arid land can act as an effective profit-maximising agent. Surely this peasant can also grow other crops instead of beet. IANSA is both a monopsonist and a monopolist; its excessive profits should be passed on to consumers and poor farmers. The specific tariff on sugar imports should be revised downwards periodically, with a view to it becoming eventually extinct. Possibly one of the reasons why this anachronism survives is that it represents an almost unique point of encounter between two (still) powerful lobbies, the peasantist one and the pro-manufacturing one, in an unholy alliance to exploit the domestic consumer.

Furthermore, sugar may be only the worst case in a long list of examples of excessive protection to domestic food production. In an open economy, food items are tradeables and domestic food prices are not expected to rise any more than international food prices. However, during the 12-month period ending in July 1991, the consumer price index rose by 24 per cent, but food prices rose by 29 per cent. The price band (which determines the limits of fluctuation for the guaranteed domestic price) for wheat in 1992 will represent a 4 per cent fall in relation to 1991, against a drop of 30 per cent in the international price. Only the poor and those who are victims of the operation of non-competitive markets or of other forms of market failure should be shielded from the discipline of the marketplace, but not large, efficient commercial farmers or powerful firms in the agro-industrial or forestry sectors.

11.5 THE EQUITY ASPECT OF GOVERNMENT EXPENDITURE

Among the many interesting questions raised by the illuminating surveys of Christopher Scott (Chapter 7) there is an extremely important one concerning the equity aspect of INDAP credit. As Scott points out, this credit was, among other forms of government expenditure, particularly progressive in terms of income redistribution. However, 50 per cent of INDAP credit in 1968 still went to farmers earning more than 2 minimum wages. Some wealthy farmers took advantage of INDAP credit in 1968. The official conditions (low personal income and assets, including land) were not really a problem; a farmer could put all his assets under his wife's name. Agricultural land and equipment, and other farm production assets, were worth very little anyway, threatened as they were by expropriation, illegal takeover and political uncertainty. Given the highly subsidised nature of INDAP credit, it would simply have been silly not to take advantage of it. The upper limit of 12 b.i.h., according to which farmers who owned more were not entitled to apply for INDAP support, was established only under Pinochet, not before.

There is thus a high probability that subsidised INDAP credit, in 1968 and after, may have failed to reach the poorest among the peasant population, and that a large share of this credit was diverted towards higher income farmers. This problem has always affected most items of social fiscal expenditure and it has proved very difficult to solve. In 1991 the Minister of Planning, Sergio Molina, announced that 60 per cent of the tax increases imposed by the Aylwin government were reaching the poor. But these tax rises were introduced with the explicit purpose of devoting new resources to health, education and housing for the poor. So the particular allocation of these funds in 1991 can be considered a success only with reference to the rather depressing experience of other attempts at helping those at the bottom of the income distribution pyramid. For other instances of items of social fiscal expenditure designed for the poor, but effectively largely received by the middle sectors and the rich in the 1980s, see Rosende (1989). This particular feature of the allocation of public sector resources may have strengthened the support for the Christian Democratic Party in 1990–1 among its traditional constituency in the middle sectors, but it is unlikely to solve the more pressing problems of the poorest.

Moreover, the strong statistical association between INDAP credit and the use of chemical fertiliser and/or improved seed, which is clearly present in the Scott data, may be seen in a completely different light. It may be the result, not of the fact that credit is a prerequisite for the use of modern inputs, but of the fact that both credit and these inputs were used, in 1968 and in 1986, by the most entrepreneurial (or wealthy) farmers. And this is not incompatible with the fact that credit was insufficient and it had to be rationed. Just as the wealthier farmers (and the middle sectors and the rich in urban areas and activities) could use other aspects of the state apparatus for their own advantage, possibly they could also use their influence to obtain a good position in the queue for rural credit, or to jump the queue altogether.

In the same way in which the IANSA sugar beet programme may not be the best way of subsidising rural employment, traditional INDAP practices may not be the most economical form of helping poor peasants. The social cost of INDAP in the late 1960s and early 1970s, 5000 officials plus all the required support infrastructure, in order to help up to 50 000 farmers, was quite high, possibly almost as much as sending every farmer to a full-time course in a university.

11.6 BY WAY OF CONCLUSIONS TO THE CONCLUSIONS

The Aylwin government has been reasonably successful in its twin objectives for the agrarian sector of preserving the most enlightened economic policies inherited from the Pinochet regime, and guaranteeing their social legitimacy by strengthening democratic practices and improving income distribution. The aims of continuity and legitimacy have been correctly identified as the only possible basis for further agricultural development. However, it would be extremely misleading to suggest that all the questions have been answered and all the problems solved. The substitution of actual profits (*renta efectiva*) for estimated profits (*renta presunta*) as the basis for farm taxation in 1990–1 may well prove to be a step backwards. It was argued by opponents of the estimated profits regime that profit estimates in the past had been smaller than actual profits. But this could have been easily solved without switching to a system with higher administrative costs and in which the possibilities of evasion and fraud are larger, as is the case with *renta efectiva*. There are limits to how far the Aylwin government and future democratic administrations in the 1990s can rely on the operation of NGOs. The main lesson to be learnt from the experience of this operation has to do with avoiding the mistakes committed by NGOs during the authoritarian period.

On the other hand, despite warnings from different sectors and observers, the promises offered by continuing and expanding national participation in international markets still seem to be larger than the respective dangers and risks. But questions of market failure, product diversification, quality control, development and diffusion of new technologies, and marketing strategies, will continue to haunt export efforts. There are also many unresolved problems in the area of equity in the distribution of gains from the operation of the free-market model. Satisfactory results in the external sector accounts depend largely on being capable of maintaining the macroeconomic balances (Hojman, 1990a; 1992). In this connection the Chilean case has been for many years exemplary in the Latin American context. However, almost two years after taking office, the Aylwin administration was still struggling against excessive appreciation of the domestic currency, a problem which was, paradoxically, provoked precisely by the great success in encouraging traditional and non-traditional exports, and foreign investment, and in generating business confidence.

Something similar could be said of poverty, and of the operation of the labour market. In mid-1991 Minister Sergio Molina announced that the incidence of poverty had fallen from 38 to 34 per cent of the population during the previous four years. Good as the outcome presented by Molina is, obviously it is not good enough. At this rate of progress (1 per cent of the population per year), poverty will not be eliminated until the year 2025. The scourge of poverty will remain a barrier to social equality and to the individual progress of a large share of the population for a long time, and certainly it will still be a problem in the mid-1990s, let alone an issue in the 1993 elections. Incidentally, the Molina figures for 1987 may not be compatible with those more pessimistic ones offered by María Elena Cruz for extreme poverty in 1983 in Chapter 1 in this volume (see also Chapter 7 by Christopher Scott). An alternative, and quite different, estimate of rural poverty has been recently provided by the Director of INDAP, Hugo Ortega (an Aylwin government appointee, and previously a senior researcher in a NGO). According to him, 2 million poor lived in rural areas in 1991, but among them only 350 000 would have been destitute. This amounts to less than 3 per cent of the national population.

It is not clear that the increases in the legal minimum wage in 1990 and 1991 will help the poor. They may actually increase unemployment, informality and marginality, and reduce participation in the labour market (Paredes and Riveros, 1989; Chacra, 1990). These resources possibly would have done more for their intended beneficiaries if they had been devoted to finance training programmes for the unskilled. The 1990–1 changes to the 1979 Labour Law, together with the potential threat of increased worker and union militancy, have generated changes in all the relevant parameters in the labour market schedules, in the wrong direction. During the 1980s, recovery after the 1982–3 crisis took place with output elasticities of employment as high as 0.8, but this elasticity had fallen to 0.4 by 1990, and it was even lower in more recent periods. Not only has the output elasticity of employment fallen, but substitution of capital for labour has been encouraged, and the incremental capital–output ratio of the economy has increased. The trade-off between employment and inflation (the Phillips curve) has deteriorated (Hojman, 1990c, 1990d; Hojman and Ramsden, 1991). (All these ratios between two variables may be misleading because they fail to take into account other related movements and relationships.) The slower pace of employment creation means also an increase in labour productivity. New jobs are not being created as fast as before, but real earnings are improving more rapidly. At least in some industries and activities, the improvement in job tenure conditions may encourage training and the development of new skills. Still, the data seem to confirm – once again – that good intentions are not sufficient: if not supported by sound policies, the impact on potential beneficiaries may well end up by being counterproductive.

References

Chacra, V. (1990) 'Efectos del salario mínimo: aplicación del método Tobit', *Cuadernos de Economía*, vol. 27 no. 80 (April) pp. 83–101.

Coloma, F. (1987) 'Crear empleo, una tarea urgente', in Larraín, F. (ed.), *Desarrollo económico en democracia* (Santiago: Universidad Católica).

Corbo, V. and Meller, P. (1982) 'The substitution of labour, skill, and capital: its implications for trade and employment', in A. O. Krueger (ed.), *Trade and employment in developing countries. Vol. 2: Factor supply and substitution* (Chicago: University of Chicago Press).

Cox, M. (1988) 'Bases de un programa para el desarrollo sostenido y equitativo del agro chileno', paper presented to the GIA–CLACSO International Conference on Latin American Agriculture, Punta de Tralca (1–4 September).

Cox, M. and Chateauneuf, R. (eds) (1988) *Potencial y políticas para el desarrollo agrícola en Chile* (Santiago: CED).

Cruz, J. M. (1988) 'La fruticultura de exportación: una experiencia de desarrollo empresarial', *Colección Estudios CIEPLAN*, vol. 25 (December) pp. 79–114.

Gómez, S. and Echeñique, J. (1986) 'Nuevos empresarios y empresas agrícolas en Chile', Documento de Trabajo, no. 277 (Santiago: FLACSO).

Hojman, D. E. (1990a) 'Chile after Pinochet: Aylwin's Christian Democrat economic policies for the 1990s', *Bulletin of Latin American Research*, vol. 9, no. 1, pp. 25–47.

Hojman, D. E. (1990b) 'What makes Chilean agriculture tick? Estimation and interpretation of elasticities in representative markets', in D. E. Hojman (ed.), *Neo-liberal Agriculture in Rural Chile* (London: Macmillan).

Hojman, D. E. (1990c) 'Employment- and earnings-generating potential of the neo-liberal model', in D. E. Hojman (ed.), *Neo-liberal Agriculture in Rural Chile* (London: Macmillan).

Hojman, D. E. (1990d) 'Employment and the labour market', paper presented to the CERC–ILAS–St Antony's College Conference on the Transition to Democracy in Chile (Liverpool) (December).

Hojman, D. E. (1992) *Chile: the political economy of development and democracy in the 1990s* (London: Macmillan).

Hojman, D. E. and Ramsden, M. (1991) 'Political change, business confidence, and the labour market' (Liverpool: ILAS) (typescript).

Inter American Development Bank (1986) *Commodity export prospects of Latin America* (Washington, D.C.: IDB).

Inter American Development Bank (1987) *Commodity export prospects of Latin America* (Washington, D.C.: IDB).

Montero, C. (1990) 'La evolución del empresariado chileno: surge un nuevo actor?', *Colección Estudios CIEPLAN*, vol. 30 (December) pp. 91–122.

Paredes, R. and Riveros, L. (1989) 'Sesgo de selección y efecto de los salarios mínimos', *Cuadernos de Economía*, vol. 26, no. 79 (December) pp. 367–83.

Rosende, F. (1989) 'Elementos para el diseño de un marco analítico en el estudio de la pobreza y distribución del ingreso en Chile', *Estudios Públicos*, vol. 34 (Autumn) pp. 5–52.

Schultz, T. W. (1968) 'The economics of Chilean agriculture', in his *Economic Growth and Agriculture* (New York: McGraw-Hill).

Valdivia, V. (1988) 'La remolacha', in Cox, M. and Chateauneuf, R. (eds), *Potencial y políticas para el desarrollo agrícola en Chile* (Santiago: CED).

Index

193